Wordpress

Build and Master Professional Looking Website

(A Definitive Guide to Building Custom Websites Using Wordpress)

Calvin Conway

Published By **Tyson Maxwell**

Calvin Conway

Wordpress: Build and Master Professional Looking Website (A Definitive Guide to Building Custom Websites Using Wordpress)

ISBN 978-1-998927-51-7

Legal & Disclaimer

The information contained in this book is not designed to replace or take the place of any form of medicine or professional medical advice. The information in this book has been provided for educational & entertainment purposes only.

The information contained in this book has been compiled from sources deemed reliable, and it is accurate to the best of the Author's knowledge; however, the Author cannot guarantee its accuracy and validity and cannot be held liable for any errors or omissions. Changes are periodically made to this book. You must consult your doctor or get professional medical advice before using any of the suggested remedies, techniques, or information in this book.

Table Of Contents

Chapter 1: What Is Wordpress?

WordPress is an open-deliver tool used for the improvement and control of internet web websites. The open-supply software program program utility development model now not only allows others to test the code behind the system, but gives get proper of entry to for modifications and redistribution. It is a loose content material material material manage tool, which possesses an smooth to apply System and particular blogging competencies that makes it one of the simplest blogging and

internet website online content material management device (CMS) in life these days.

It is written with PHP and runs on a MySQL database, granting customers infinite area and contents for numerous makes use of. It is price-effective, gives the last social media integration for a great industrial, without issues upgraded, and handy to apply.

WordPress is an amazing net web site platform that gives a number of options at the kind of net net websites that might be

created, with examples starting from e-commerce to enterprise company to journey, fashion, photos, and membership net internet websites. Its gadget is bendy and malleable, granting the man or woman a big workspace with hundreds of splendid abilties.

Difference among WordPress.Com and

WordPress.Org

Generally, WordPress offers sorts of company net website hosting; Blogs and Websites. If you had decided to create a blog, you probably knew that you have been furnished alternatives -

WordPress.Org and WordPress.Com. Your desire many of the 2 depends on what you require.

WordPress.Com

WordPress.Com is the proper choice at the same time as you do not need to host the internet site manually. WordPress.Com gives hosting services, and genuinely, that is without trouble the right way to be happy with taking walks a weblog without price. WordPress.Com is an top notch desire in case you need to release your weblog or be diagnosed the usage of a WordPress weblog right away and with little to no paintings or value.

You can discover more than one limitations to this alternative. A WordPress.Com website is difficult to adjust because of the reality there is a restricted preference of subject matters, and also you can't add your commercials.

It can be a horrible opportunity if you intend to earn some coins using your blog.

The very last component which you have to be reminded of is which you do now not have possession of the weblog; nice WordPress owns the weblog. WordPress can close down your internet net site at any duration in case you fail to satisfy its coverage.

WordPress.Org

WordPress.Org may be very bendy, however at a rate: you require a site name further to an internet hosting to host your blog.

Also, this isn't a excessive quantity. Hosting portions usually begin at a few dollars every 30 days.

Implementing this approach gives for extra freedom as you have got get right of access to to the hassle matter you want, and you may extend your blog's talents with plenty of plugins at your disposal, on the aspect of in addition functionality in your blog.

If you had meant or envisage to create a blog or net website for your agency, then this feature is a much higher desire.

There are many alternatives online for net website hosting, at very inexpensive charges

Why select out WordPress?

There is a package of motives why you ought to choose WordPress to make your internet web site or weblog.

☐ Firstly, it is opensupply software program application application. It technique you are not needed to pay for a license to utilize it.

☐ It is accessible to apply. Not just in terms of set up and configurations, however it moreover does not require any technical recognise-a way to form and maintain the content material material fabric.

☐ It could be very flexible and without troubles conforms in your requirements. The default configuration contains the most critical subjects, and you can increase WordPress the use of many new and influential plugins.

☐ WordPress has recorded an eight- 12% worldwide usage.

Thousands of net sites are run on WordPress floor

from numerous sources; this indicates that it's miles a depended on software software across the world.

☐ It is continuously being superior. The system has many builders strolling together to enable WordPress to enhance generally, and with every update, it's miles extra stable, higher, and greater man or woman-friendly!

☐ WordPress offers you the option of gaining access to remarks and comments. As the ones are valuable assets of information, your readers, prospective customers, and traffic offer you, permitting you to enhance in plenty of procedures.

☐ When you personal your very very non public WordPress web net web page, you manipulate all the content for your internet site, and you could construct your take into account and authority for your precise address on the internet.

☐ It Increases web web page site visitors for your website. Doing this can growth readership and allows you construct your emblem. Blogging with WordPress offers you the manner to connect with the proper readers, which require your answers and offerings.

☐ WordPress actions flawlessly with social media allowing you to without hassle promote and percent new content material material to love-minded human beings throughout a massive amount of numerous social media networks in the course of the entire global net.

In summary, WordPress may be very patron-best and easy for beginners. It offers a tremendous form of alternatives on a manner to control your content material cloth material and customise your internet web page on line. WordPress is probably an great choice in terms of the appearance of a net web website online or blog and allows you sell your content cloth to masses of heaps the world over.

Make sure that in advance than you start the installation, you have got a easy view of your plans on your net web page. If you want some time, that is in reality first-class. Outline what it's far your web net web page want for use for, a manner to ensure it reaches its complete ability, a way to gain a big target audience with its contents.

You cannot rush perfection. So take a 2d to realise the big picture of your dream and watch all of it payout at the same time as you grow to be with a brilliant internet net page.

Chapter 2: Installing Wordpress

Before we get to installing a modern-day WordPress, when you have already were given one but would really like to start all yet again from scratch, you need to delete the pre-installed content material fabric.

There are techniques as a way to do this;

First, strive (Clean Uninstall)

1. Erase all of the WordPress folders and files that belong to you out of your internet internet site (that is generally from the ' public_html'

list).

2. Next, absolutely erase the WordPress database table and purchaser (happens via the control panel (CPanel) if this segment exists for your internet web site). Head to MySQL, that is the database vicinity, and now, the database and clients may be removed from the interface.

3. Now you are prepared to install your WordPress.

Second strive (Rapid Fix Uninstall)

1. Erase the WordPress database desk and man or woman.

2. Form a latest database desk and character and preserve to replace the ' wp-config.Php' record with a few thing in addition records you could have, you can alternatively use the right patron name further to desk name from the previous database once more.

three. You can now run the WordPress installer by means of way of organising your internet site on line.

How to Erase WordPress Folders and Files

You can erase your WordPress files on the equal time as utilising the following strategies:

• Log into your internet web page's cPanel and visit the file browser. Locate the folder containing the whole WordPress documents and delete the files.

• Log into your net web page with FTP software software (as an instance, FileZilla). Find the folder wherein the installation of WordPress was stored. Choose the files and folders, then click on the delete preference and verify the removal.

Now on your new WordPress. There are many approaches to install WordPress. However, the most efficient method is thru the Cpanel of your hosting company.

Cpanel is a segment of your website hosting account that offers crucial aids that assist you in handling everything that your host is attached to - from the net internet page it is associated with, to your emails. Within this area, you can set up several apps and take care of a whole lot of houses concerning your host and region. You can log in at http://yourdomainname.

com/cpanel.

The WordPress set up hyperlink is pretty like below a section titled: Software or Services or Softaculous App Installer.

Once you have got located it, click the WordPress icon in this section and take a look at the ones subsequent steps carefully.

☐ Click the installation tab at the identical time because the WordPress records internet internet web page opens up and continue to fill inside the required statistics beneath. You need to make sure that at this issue, you understand what it's far you need to make; a blog or a website, and moreover you need to have already picked out a name on your net website or blog.

index-18_1.Jpg

☐ Next, choose your protocol; this is not essential, so in case you do no longer understand what it is, you can go away it as it's far.

☐ Choose the region you would like to install under.

☐The subsequent vicinity will ask you to pick out a list; this can be left easy except you need to location inside the WordPress in a sub-list, it truly is sincerely the location of your region name, like .Com, .Org, .Weblog. You most probable need to go away it with the inspiration listing of your vicinity, in order that space must be left by myself.

If you scroll down similarly, you may see every different set of data questions; this precise location pertains to the internet website online on-line you want to make and your get right of entry to as an admin (proprietor and operator of the net web site.)

☐ Fill on your net website name and description.

☐ There is a checkbox asking in case your internet website need to be made part of a multisite. You need to depart it unchecked except you would love to run a couple of WordPress net websites from a unmarried installation.

☐ Then, pick out out out an admin call and password. The default admin name is ' admin,' and technically, it's far much less complicated to don't forget, however it would greater first-class as a way to invent a trendy one, due to the fact the default one makes it smooth as a manner to get hacked. The system can also generate a robust password for you, however the ones are greater tough to recollect. When customizing yours, ensure to feature numbers and symbols, keeping an eye at the strength meter, so that you comprehend on the equal time as it is ideal sufficient.

☐ Insert your e mail cope with (the best you actively use, virtually in case you have many to pick out from) and make

certain to do not forget this one and all of the previous facts you added on this section. A accurate e mail address is vital because of the fact if you come what can also forgot your password, WordPress could send you a reset link for your email, so be careful. Choose a language you select too.

☐ For protection features, you may decide to restrict the amount of login attempts. The opportunity exists as a checkbox, and you have to handiest choose this in case you are absolutely and completely certain that you could no longer ever neglect about any of your login statistics; this can not be forced enough, because of the fact there's nothing pretty like the feeling of trying to benefit get right of entry to to a few factor that belongs to you and being locked out. After all, you can't don't forget an appropriate information. Make first-rate you are sure in case you pick out to apply this option.

☐ The advanced options can be skipped till you're a complex client, and you can pass right ahead and click on ' installation.'

index-21_1.Jpg

This must take a few minutes, so sit down lower back, loosen up, and get geared up to paintings with one of the coolest and maximum accessible content manage systems you've got ever seen.

Getting to understand the perks of being an Admin

The subsequent step after installing your WordPress might be to discover ways to find your way at some stage in the admin location.

The first trouble you must understand is that WordPress operates from sides; the Frontend and Backend. They are

sides of the same coin, and that they paintings together that will help you nicely make your net website. One of them is used to control your content material cloth, and the possibility is used to show that content fabric.

The Frontend is the precept internet web web page, the element seen to the users. It is in which all your content material cloth cloth goes while you upload it, mainly which includes your web site design and the pages, menus, and media you area there for an give up-character.

The Backend refers back to the admin place, wherein you can manage all the net internet website contents; this is in which authorized clients (clients who you have selected to provide access to) can log in and make vital changes and deletions to the contents at the web web website online like which encompass posts and pages, selecting a topic depend, including plugins, developing navigation menus, placing widgets and so forth, also called the Content Management System (CMS) location.

To get entry to and navigate to the admin location, visithttp://yourdomainname.Com/wpadmin (make certain to insert

your

actual

area

name

in

vicinity

of

yourdomainname)

or

http://yoursitename.Com/wp-

login.Php and login with the all of the information that you

used even as you fill within the required fields earlier than installing WordPress.

If you log in and what you are seeing is the the front-give up - the residence internet web page of your net web site - you can rapid move to the backend by way of the usage of clicking the call of your internet web site inside the

' admin bar.' that is the toolbar on the top of every net internet page with a black background and a few menu gadgets.

As your internet website online keeps to increase and increase, the admin vicinity turns into a pal to you. So take it sluggish to research all you can about that surroundings and get used to all of the functions.

The dashboard and its makes use of

Now which you have decided your manner into the admin location, what lies earlier than you is your dashboard. Think of the dashboard as a few thing of a hallway or corridor with loads of doors on each side. Through this hallway, you've got get entry to to all elements of your house.

The equal goes for the dashboard. This space offers you all that you want to edit, add, create and delete any content fabric, set up scenario matters and plugins, assign roles to clients, manage and customise your internet web page, it all first-class a click on on on away. It is the number one internet page that welcomes you into the magic of content cloth cloth control.

The dashboard is divided into precise sections, every with its particular uses. If you would like an opportunity layout, you can constantly trade the shortcuts later to suit your choice.

☐ Dashboard Menu This phase of WordPress provides you with a navigation menu that includes multiple menu options, which encompass media, posts, pages, library, appearance alternatives, feedback, users, plugins, a few settings, and tool on the opportunity aspect; this is mainly targeted at the contents of your net website.

☐ Screen Options - The dashboard has numerous forms of widgets contained inner it, which might be every displayed or hid on a few shows. It includes checkboxes to cover or show alternatives approximately what can be visible at the show and moreover offers you the functionality to carry out person customization on a few areas at the display display of the admin.

☐ Welcome - This, of path, includes the Customize Your Site desire, which lets you alter your WordPress challenge count. The column in the centre offers some of the beneficial and useful links, which consist of developing a web web page, creating a weblog located up, and seeing the the the front give up of your net website online. The final column has hyperlinks to menus, widgets, settings of feedback, similarly to a hyperlink that directs you to the First Steps With WordPress internet net web page at some point of the WordPress codex.

☐ Quick Draft- This is a smaller located up editor that lets in you to write down, shop, and publish a publish from the dashboard of the admin. Quick Draft includes some notes concerning the draft, the selected choose out for the draft, and later, it's going to probable be saved as a draft.

☐ WordPressNews The WordPress News is a widget that indicates the modern-day records, which includes the contemporary software program software model, alerts, updates, news about the software program application, all from WordPress's decent weblog.

☐ Activity - This widget consists of the currently published remarks to your blog, posts made currently, and the modern-day published posts. It lets you to each approve or

index-26_1.Jpg

disapprove, edit, reply, or put off a comment, as well as deliver a statement to direct mail.

☐ Take a Glance- This factor provides a big overview of your blog's posts, the amount of posts efficiently posted, in addition to pages, and the kind of feedback; while any of those hyperlinks are clicked, you may be directed to their display in which the records have end up gotten from. It moreover displays the model of WordPress that is presently walking, together with the presently active difficulty recall on the internet web page.

Chapter 3: Customizing Your Website Or Blog Net Web Web Page

Before your net internet site online can function because it should be, it has to undergo some modifications that might allow it to deliver your content material better; this entails making the whole use of the content fabric control system of WordPress.

The first direction of movement might be to get nicely familiar with the General Settings segment; that is used to exercising session the smooth configuration settings of your website. To get to this component, you click on on on settings after which today's.

Listed and defined beneath are the fields contained on this place.

☐ Site Title: This shows the call of the internet site online inside the template header.

☐ Tagline: It is for showing a brief sentence about your net web page. See the tagline because the internet internet page's motto, one-line bait, hook, and line for potential traffic.

☐ WordPress Address (URL): This is the URL of the WordPress listing where all your center application documents may be decided.

☐ Site Address (URL): In this discipline, you can enter the net website on line URL that you would like your net web web page to expose on the browser.

☐ Email Address: This asks on your email deal with, which aids you in recuperating your password and offers information approximately any available replace.

☐ Membership: This function once enabled - gives the ability for any involved person to test in and create an account in your internet internet page.

☐ New User Default Position: This is the default function set for a newly registered person or member.

☐ Timezone: Helps you pick out a time sector primarily based in town of your preference.

☐ Date Format: Selects the date layout of your choice to be shown on the internet site on line.

☐ Time Format: This detail offers with the time format which you require to be tested at the net internet site online.

☐ Week Starts On: Here, you can pick out out the weekday that you favor to begin the beginning of a brand new week to your WordPress calendar. Monday is the default set day.

☐ Site Language: Appoints a language of your desire for the WordPress dashboard.

index-30_1.Jpg

Once you're finished and are happy along side your options, make sure to click on on the store adjustments button at the lowest of the sector.

General writing and reading settings

Two crucial factors come into play every time the idea of a internet website online is brought up. That is reading and writing.

Major contents of the internet website or weblog are in phrases which might be to be take a look at with the aid of the usage of the viewer and with out suitable traits being decided on. The writing settings come up with the threat to govern your writing enjoy for the

higher and gives you first rate options for customizing your internet site, offering reliable competencies that help with enhancing and together with posts, pages, or perhaps sorting outpost types. It moreover includes a few optional functions along aspect; posting thru email, remote publishing, and replace services.

To get right of entry to this section, head to the settings section all over again and click on on writing. There you can discover a place contain precise residences to help make your writing greater thrilling.

Formatting: In this challenge, alternatives provide a extra exciting revel in for the character.

The first, that is convert emoticons which incorporates :-) and:-P to photos on show, can flip textual content emoticons to seen emoticons.

The other opportunity, this is; WordPress, will accurate XHTML nestled untenably, automatically adjusting something invalid XHTML turn out to be placed inside the pages or the posts.

Default Post Category: This is a category which can exercise to any put up, and if you need, it may be left Uncategorized.

Default Post Format: It is made use of with the useful resource of topics to pick a particular positioned up format which can have a observe to any put up, or you can create numerous styles for various forms of jobs.

Post thru email: For this option, your e-mail information is used to make posts and positioned up posts on your weblog thru email. To lease this, you'll be required to form an unique electronic mail that possesses POP3 access - which handiest you may use, and some thing mail this cope with receives is going to be posted.

Mail Server: This allows the e-mails that you transferred to WordPress to be have a look at by using you and keeps them for later series. To use this option, you require a Mail Server well suited with POP3, and it will very own a URI (Uniform Resource Identifier) contact information that have to be entered there.

Login Name: To shape posts, your WordPress calls for an e-mail account particularly for this reason. The call of the login will hire this electronic mail cope with, and you should strive as an entire lot as you could to preserve undisclosed, as spammers will share the links, so that it will redirect to their web sites.

Password: You will want to assign a password for the over email cope with. Do your wonderful to ensure that it's miles strong.

Default Mail Category: This lets in you to pick out out a especially made business enterprise for the entire posts that are published using the feature of Post by means of e-mail.

Update Services: What this option does is to tell the internet site online's replace services whenever you add a modern-day publish.

Take a check the Update Services codex for the listing of services.

Once another time, ensure to click on the Save Changes preference when you are accomplished.

In terms of reading, the patron's comfort is what subjects, in addition to what is extra on hand for you with reference to uploading content. Reading settings are used to adjust the abilties of the web page on the the the the front and also can trade the range of posts to be validated on the primary page.

To choose your desire for studying tendencies, head over to settings, and click on on analyzing. On that net page, the following options can be visible;

Frontpage indicates: This place is used to view the the the front net page in one of the following codecs:

Your modern-day-day posts: This shows the these days uploaded posts on the front web net page.

A static internet page: It indicates the static pages on the the front internet web page.

Front Page: Here, you can choose the particular web page you want to show at the the front (domestic) net web page from the drop-down.

Posts Page: With this feature, you may select out the page from the drop-down, which incorporates posts.

Blog pages show at maximum: This is the variety of posts which is probably to be displayed consistent with web page or website on-line. The default quantity of pages is prepared at 10.

Syndication feeds display the maximum present day: With this option, the user can see the fashion of posts contemporary each time they select to down load one of the net page feeds. 10 is the default variety.

For every article in a feed, display: This area is used to show the put up through manner of selecting any of the following codecs: Full Text: This suggests the whole placed up absolutely. It is ready because the default choice.

Summary: It shows a quick assessment of the put up you created.

Search Engine Visibility: In the occasions which you click on in this checkbox, it technique you have decided on to hide your content material cloth from engines like google like google, because it discourages them from indexing your internet net web page. So your internet website on line will pass ignored with the useful resource of on-line serps.

Tweaking the discussions and media settings to suit your flavor

Discussion in phrases of WordPress may be seen due to the fact the touch among the net page's blogger and the site visitors/clients.

The developer executes those configurations to have manipulate of posts or pages acquired from customers.

This region is critical to bloggers. If you planned to utilize WordPress as a Content Management System, this element is a whole lot much less critical for you.

To get to the settings, head to the settings section and click on on on talk. These are the fields which may be on that net internet web page; Default content material settings: These are the default settings for the ones new pages, honestly new posts you can create. Three more settings are contained internal this: Try to alert any blogs connected to from the content material fabric: Whenever an article is published, a notification (sends trackback and pings) is despatched to exceptional web sites and blogs. If you submit content material cloth containing links to new blogs inside it, your blog will try to alert those wonderful blogs to inform them of the

reality that you connected to them (and you published a content fabric). The stop quit end result of this may be in an automatic declaration at the weblog (the period you pick out out this feature).

Allow hyperlink notifications from other blogs (pingbacks and trackbacks): This choice lets in you to take pings from severa blogs. The length that particular blogs connect to you, and that they offer you with a warning; they will write an automated statement.

You can unmark this placing in order no longer to put up these remarks.

Let humans post remarks on glowing content material material fabric: You might also decide whether or no longer to permit exceptional people to comment on the object with this putting; this offers your web site traffic the risk to offer your article with comments.

You ought to adjust the settings in line with what you require for special character posts.

More Comment Settings: This setting possesses the alternatives underneath:

Comment creator is remitted to fill the spaces for call and e mail: If this container is chosen, it becomes a need to for internet site site visitors to offer of their e mail address and contact. So,

every time an person leaves a statement, they'll ought to fill a subject requiring them to depart inside the once more of their e-mail cope with and phone.

Users are mandated to be registered and logged in earlier than commenting: If you pick out this option, most effective site visitors which is probably registered can depart within the again of any comments inside the shape of comments; if left unchecked, anyone should go away some thing quantity of remarks.

Note: If you choose this option, your readers first need to log in earlier than writing a comment. For the bulk of blogs, it is maximum widely recognized no longer to affirm this option.

Automatically forestall remarks on articles older than --

days: This preference offers you a time body for accepting remarks beneath a selected put up. When you choose this alternative, your website site visitors can be not able to location comments after the big fashion of days you've got unique. Ensure to go away sufficient time in your readers to put in writing a commentary if you choose to use this option.

Enable threaded feedback: When you select this very alternative, clients ought to have a discussion or leave a reply and accumulate feedback. If you choose out this feature, analyzing

remarks internal (responses to comments) distinctive comments may be more sincere.

Divide comments into pages with excessive-degree remarks on every internet page and the internet page proven thru default: In the occasion of your pages receiving numerous remarks, you may divide them amongst wonderful pages with the useful resource of technique of selecting this region; this may bring about WordPress splitting contents with greater than a specific type of top-stage remarks in a couple of pages.

Comments may be shown with the remarks above each internet net web page: This function allows you put together the remarks in an ascending or falling order shape. You can choose out whether or now not or not you would really like each the older or newer remarks to be seen first. It is not unusual for optimum bloggers to pick out out to reveal the current feedback.

Email me whenever: This putting has two opportunities, which may be:

Any man or woman posts a statement: If this feature is chosen, the writer might be sent an email if and while a commentary is posted - for each remark posted. When checked,

you could get keep of an email on every occasion a person places a new commentary.

A statement is saved for moderation: This degree exists in case you do not want a commentary to had been up to date before the admin has a hazard to slight. If decided on, you could get an email while an character posts a modern assertion that is being stored for looking. The remarkable element to do might be to pick out out out each the ones alternatives, as it is the exceptional manner to stay updated with new feedback.

Before a remark showing: This putting offers, you get right of get admission to to to how the posts are well managed. Within this option lies different settings:

A comment ought to be manually authorized: If this concern is checked, first-class the feedback approved via way of the admin has a risk to be seen on the pages or the pages. When a modern-day comment is submitted, it needs to be everyday with the useful useful resource of an administrator.

Comment writer need to have a previously popular remark: This need to be decided on if you will favor to obtain remarks from a selected writer who left a

statement and whose e-mail records is much like that of the formerly posted commentary. Otherwise, the message need to be taken for moderation.

If a person locations the first remark, you need to signify this comment. Then, the comments of that particular patron can be displayed without any want for approval.

Comment Moderation: This includes most effective a pleasant specific quantity of hyperlinks which can be given get right of access to to remark. A remark can be held within the queue if it has some amount of links (that is to make certain via you). There is also have a location supplied in an effort to fill in terms. Insert one word in each line. When a statement has those phrases, it's far stored and queued for moderation.

Comment Blacklist: Here, you may insert junk mail phrases of your desire, which you rather now not determine for your clients to function inside the remarks, email, or URL. Later, the terms you have got have been given decided on is probably filtered within the feedback. You can fill in terms in the issue, one word, or IP consistent with line. Whenever the device comes in the course of a declaration containing any of these terms, it's far seen as junk mail.

Avatars: An avatar is simplest a small picture this is displayed in the nook on the proper upside the dashboard panel, proper next for your call. An avatar is known as a picture that goes with you amongst weblogs, showing near your name at the same time as you comment on internet internet sites with avatar viewing settings enabled. It is your profile photograph.

Within this option, you pick out to allow showing of avatars for folks who touch upon your net site.

Avatar Display: This feature suggests your avatar subsequent in your call whilst it's miles checked.

Maximum score: Four top notch avatar alternatives to be had for your features. These are G, PG, R, and X. This is prepared the age variety in that you pick in terms of what audience may be granted get proper of access to on your posts.

Default Avatar: Within this preference, several more variances of avatars with snap shots are contained; and that they may be saved following your purchaser's e-mail touch data.

When you are completed, make certain that click on on the Save Changes icon.

Media Settings

In the Media Settings internet web page, you are allowed to set most snap shots length delivered into the placed up content. These settings assist you preserve time in case you may continuously select pix to hold the ideal duration or would love to utilize the default settings for massive and medium image sizes. The Uploading files opportunity offers you the capability to pick out out whether or not or not your contents are prepared internal a 12 months and month primarily based absolutely folder.

The Media Settings net web page can be accessed thru Settings, and then you could click on on Media in the left list of options. Within the page that follows up, you may configure some default settings for media (specifically images) you need to add.

Chapter 4: How To Nicely Manipulate Your Contents

Contents inside WordPress is normally controlled and created using a WYSIWYG editor. The WYSIWYG

(recommended as wiz-ee-wig and is an acronym for 'what you observe is what you get') editor is used to adjust the contents of posts and pages, concurrently allowing the writer to appearance what it'll seem like as a completed product.

This feature is referred to as a live preview, and it permits you spot your content cloth fabric exactly how your views will see it afterward. It is based on Microsoft Word to keep topics easy.

Despite its simplicity, it does now not lack in features, offering buttons with useful capabilities that carry out obligations like; putting a delegated textual content in ambitious, locations a particular text in italic, actions (cancels out) decided on textual content, creates an unordered list, creates an ordered listing, places selected textual content as a quote, aligns text left, aligns text middle, aligns text proper, inserts a link and gets rid of a link.

index-45_1.Jpg

Some others embody; a tag that inserts 'more,' a spell checker, a button that makes the WYSIWYG-editor full display screen, indicates extra or fewer buttons, formats the chosen textual content or paragraph, underlines the chosen textual content, aligns complete textual content, selects a textual content color, pastes copied text gotten from a one in all a type software program as number one wording, inserts media, and some others.

Categories and Tags

A

massive

distinction

lies

between

WordPress

classes and WordPress tags. Categories help you organization your put up with different similar posts, however Tags are used

to create businesses that in form into a couple of classes. For instance, pets can be a class; rabbits, kittens, and puppies should form the tags.

How to form and edit classes

Categories are very important equipment used to categorise and employer your art work. They assist you installation your posts and pages under precise subjects so that they're much less complex to find.

You may additionally pick to put in writing a subject that has a massive variety of statistics but includes a piece of it on your post. If you create a category on that concern remember, you may without troubles institution a future post on that very same difficulty bear in mind in case you wrote each different.

How to create a new beauty

Building a present day magnificence is pretty sincere. Just click on on on Posts after which pick out out Categories on the menu to the left.

Within the display that looks, you can create a present day class on the left side of it, and on the proper, you may see all of your currently gift lessons.

If your WordPress have been really hooked up, there is probably pleasant one class; Uncategorized. To upload a state-of-the-art institution, you need to fill within the ones fields;

• Name: This consists of the call of your magnificence, precisely due to the fact the viewer will see it.

• Slug: It is the decision used inside the URL (this area is non-compulsory, so that you do now not want to fill this). It only consists of letters - all of which want to be decrease-case - hyphens and numbers.

• Parent: If you need to make a sub-magnificence, select a determine class (this is non-obligatory).

• Description: This consists of an outline of the magnificence you're growing concerning the posts it's miles grouping (that is non-obligatory).

After you've got crammed in all the fields with the vital information, click on at the Add New Category button. Now, your new category will appear in the right part of the display display, below the list of education you have got were given. Later, even as you upload or edit a submit, the contemporary-day elegance may also be to be had an notable way to select from.

How to outline the default category

A default magnificence is a category that a publish of the net page is routinely underneath as speedy because it has been created. If a class is not particular at the same time as including a new publish, the default magnificence can be determined on. To choose a class as your default elegance;

• Click Settings after which Writing in the left menu to open the Writing Settings show.

• Right on the Default Post phase, select out a class you need to use as a default elegance (this desires to be a category that already exists).

Note: A elegance that has been selected as a default magnificence cannot be deleted.

How do you pick out a category?

When you're writing a put up, you may select one or more categories at the right. If one isn't always picked, the default elegance will routinely be decided on.

Post tags

Unlike schooling, tags are optionally available in terms of utilization.

Especially if you are a amateur, tags can be a hint confusing. But at the equal time, they're to be had.

Tags are used to organisation, similar topics, linking them with a single phrase or phrase; consistent with post, a maximum of to three tags need to be accomplished.

How to create a today's tag:

A tag is added through the Tags show. First, choose out Posts and then Tags on the left menu. You will see a display like this;

The left part of this display is in which a brand new tag can be delivered, and the proper thing is wherein you get an outline of all the presently present tags.

To upload a modern-day tag, entire the subsequent fields:

• Name: This is the decision of your tag because it will appear to the viewer.

• Slug: The call used in the URL (an non-obligatory function)

• Description: This is an outline of the tag's houses (non-compulsory)

When you're finished filling all of the needed fields, click on the button that announces, Add New Tag; now, your new tag will appear within the proper a part of the show, subsequent to all the others you had in advance than.

It is less complicated to characteristic a brand new tag on the same time as you are developing a publish.

Within the Tag past of the positioned up, fill inside the call you selected for the tag you would like to feature. It can be created if it does now not exist already.

Chapter 5: How To Feature Contents In Your New Net Site

Posts vs. Pages

When it comes to developing and inclusive of content fabric to your WordPress internet net web page, you've got the pricey to choose among making both a positioned up or net net web page. Both of them have their makes use of and may add taken into consideration one of a type dynamic elements on your website on-line.

You need to observe that a submit is pretty unique from the web page; posts are your blog entries which is probably made now and then and are indexed in your weblog with the most current on top, at the same time as you may relate pages just like the About Us and Contact Us pages of your net net web page (default pages which have been gift whilst you established your WordPress), that are seldom created and static.

index-52_1.Jpg

How to create and update Pages

Creating Page on WordPress

Pages are typically used for static (constant) content material or widespread records, even though you can normally edit or update them whenever you want. If you're using WordPress as a Content Management System, most of your content material material might be in pages. Keep in mind that high-quality directors and editors can create or delete pages. If you would really like to view the pages presently available on your internet net page, click on on All pages from the navigation section.

New pages may be introduced via clicking on the Add New button beneath the Pages phase. Creating a modern-day-day internet page is just like creating a modern day positioned up, besides for the reality

that you can't positioned into effect tags or education for pages.

Still, pages can very own determine pages; this indicates; if you may opt to have the net internet web page as a toddler (concerning each one-of-a-kind web internet web page) of every different internet net web page, you want to indent the internet web page column in the menu segment, and it is going to be visible as a menu content material material material from the discern net page.

Ensure that a currently created web page does no longer routinely get protected in the menu. To gain this, you first should discover the Menu phase. Then encompass the internet web page to a custom menu of your preference. The Menu settings can be seen underneath Appearance inside the navigation location of the Dashboard. The web page may be inserted into the menu thru ticking the sphere on it and selecting to Add to Menu.

Some of the functions that lie inside the Pages phase are; Page Title: At the pinnacle of this display, you can select your web page name.

It is constantly feasible to modify this later in case you want to.

If you choose now not to use custom menus, then this name can also be used as a menu item internal your menu. If that is the case, the heading of the page ought to be saved brief.

Under the web page perceive, the Permalink (or URL) of the web page will appear after the page has been stored.

Adding content material fabric

Beneath the name is the area in which you may content material fabric may be inserted via the WYSIWYG-editor.

Publish

Here, you may find out the alternatives to preserve, put up, and delete your net page. Some of the alternatives for those are;

• Save Draft (button): You can shop your web page with out posting it on the net.

• Preview (button): This lets you preview your internet internet web page in your browser, even in advance than it's been finished.

• Status: This permits select the popularity (modern-day kingdom) of your internet page, each as a Draft or Pending Review.

• Visibility: You can select out who sees your web page and the way it is visible. The Visibility of the web page can each be public, password-included (clients want to supply a password to view the content material fabric), or personal (only seen for users who're logged in).

• Publish: You can select to post your age right away or select a date in order that your new net net web page may be published later.

• Move to Trash: You can waft your web page to the trash, and it could although be restored from the Trash.

• Publish (button): This button, whilst clicked, saves the net internet web page and uploads it on the net.

Page attributes

These are precise attributes that might be possessed by using pages;

• Parent: Selects the parent internet page of the current net net page. This function is vital whilst you do not outline your menu, or while you decide to apply a breadcrumb plugin.

• Template: Multiple templates are contained inner most topics; this offers you the functionality to choose out a (awesome) internet web page layout for a web page. The amount of templates varies amongst problems. Here, you could choose the template for this web web page.

• Order: In this phase, you will input numerous for ordering your pages. You ought to use this selection while your custom menu is not described. The plugin PageMash also can be used in preference to the Order opportunity, as pages may be dragged and dropped to alternate their order.

Featured picture

With the Featured picture preference, an image can be uploaded for use with that internet net page, relying on how it's miles defined inner your subject matter. For instance, numerous subjects use this feature so you will without issue be capable of choose out a header photograph or a thumbnail for one precise page; this works clearly the same manner as consisting of a ordinary image. Click the Set featured photo button at the bottom proper to set the featured photograph.

How to edit an cutting-edge internet net page

In WordPress, there are types of enhancing an internet page: a normal edit and a brief edit.

Edit a web page

• Head to the web page evaluate after choosing Pages after which All pages in the left menu.

• Now you get to collect a standard evaluation of all of your current pages. Place your cursor on a web page find out. Under that name,

some options will seem.

• Click on Edit (really clicking at the web page title is another way to edit the net web page): The decided on web web page can be opened to alter the contents and options of the net page.

• To get the internet net page offline, click on on on Status: Draft inside the Publish region at the right.

• Do not forget about about to click on at the Update button to keep the adjustments (or even the Save Draft button if the internet web page isn't organized to be published but).

Quick edit

• The initial steps are quite heaps much like the overall edit, except this time, you may click Quick Edit in region of Edit.

• The options of this web page can be altered inside this place.

After, ensure you click on on at the replace button to store the adjustments you made.

How to delete a web web page

For an internet page to be deleted, you first need to pass it to the trash. After that, the net web page can be surely deleted or restored that web page.

To circulate a web page to the trash

• Head to the web page evaluation (through deciding on Pages and then clicking All pages inside the left menu)

• Now you have have been given a show of all your pages, and subsequent, region your cursor over a web page pick out out. Under that become aware about, some options will appear: Click the Trash.

- The net page can be moved to the trash instantly.

To Restore or Delete in reality

To restore a page or to delete it completely, visit Trash and location your cursor on the net net web page name of the page you need to repair or delete virtually and click on on whatever choice you want to carry out.

How to make and control Posts

Making Your First Post

With WordPress, it is easy to launch smooth content material material thru simply consisting of new posts. If you need to make a extremely-contemporary put up, click on on at the Add New button, that is beneath the Posts section, and you will be taken to a content fabric cloth author internet web page, which seems hundreds like every regular word processor.

The content section is made available in two awesome tabs: the world of imaginative and prescient and the text view. The visual view suggests the text because it might be considered on a finished internet web page,

geared up for website on-line site visitors and users, at the same time as the text view famous the HTML format of the internet web page.

Usually, posts are typically used for strolling a blog. But you could furthermore use posts for a statistics phase to your net website.

To evaluation posts

Click on Posts inside the left menu to get a top stage view of all present posts.

How to feature a current submit

Click the Posts choice at the navigation menu and choose Add New from the left menu. Once you are completed placing a few aspect content material material you need into the sector provided for you, click on at the Publish button.

Adding content cloth

Beneath the call is the region wherein you can content material may be inserted through the WYSIWYG-editor.

Publish

Here, you may find the alternatives to preserve, placed up, and delete your net web page. Some of the alternatives for these are;

• Save Draft (button): You can preserve your net internet page without publishing it at the net.

• Preview (button): This helps you to preview your internet net web page to your browser, even in advance than it is been completed.

• Status: This permits pick the repute (modern nation) of your internet internet web page, both as a Draft or Pending Review.

• Visibility: You can choose who sees your net internet web page and the way it is seen. The visibility of your web page can each be public, Password-blanketed (users ought to deliver a password to view the content material cloth), or personal (simplest visible for clients who're logged in).

• Publish: You can pick out to place up your age right away or choose a date in order that your new page can be posted later.

• Move to Trash: You can pass your page to the trash, and it can no matter the reality that be restored from the trash.

• Publish (button): This button, at the same time as clicked, saves the net page and uploads it on the internet.

Format

In this detail, you could pick the layout of your publish. With this exciting characteristic, a blogger can alter the appearance of a manner to put up thru selecting a Post Format from

a radio-button list. There are precise put up codecs within numerous troubles.

Categories

Here you can institution your put up under one or more lessons(a topic of relation).

Tags

Here your articles can be connected through ultra-modern functions. Just enter your tag and click at the Add button. Or you could click on at the Choose from the maximum used tags link to pick out out out of your maximum currently used tags.

Posts can also have featured pix and can be moved to the trash, restored or deleted completely and edited frequently or brief, with the identical strategies as validated above in pages.

Chapter 6: Handling Your Media

The Media Library

WordPress affords you with a media library for coping with all your pictures, movies, and report uploads.

The media library may be discovered in the admin location inside the left menu.

To navigate to the media library, click on Media. Whatever media you add may be implemented in both your posts or pages or perhaps each. It is essential to understand that after you have uploaded a file (photo, video, and document) that it is now on your server (your net website on-line) and does no longer need to be uploaded once more.

Uploading into your media library

To insert a brand new media object for your library, click on on the Add New link. From this feature, add a modern picture. After

index-63_1.Jpg

your image has been uploaded, you may see it has been introduced to the library and may be accessed each time you want it.

Adding Media to a Post or a Page

Media is set up to pages and posts as visible factors that assist you hook up with all which you have been analyzing. When editing or growing an internet web page or publish, click on Add Media, that is a button decided honestly above the content cloth area.

You can consist of present media already uploaded on your net web site or upload new media. Do no longer try and add

the same record greater than as soon as as it will accumulate some greater area and upload muddle.

If it has already been uploaded, select it out of your media library.

Inserting an picture

Right above the WYSIWYG editor, there can be a button that will help you upload an image:

If this button is clicked, a window containing the following will appear.

There are 3 techniques to insert an photo:

• Upload Files: This method includes you add an image out of your computer; that is the default desire set via the machine.

• Insert from URL: If you would love to use any photo at the net, you can insert it through the URL.

• Media Library: This involves you consisting of an photograph that you had already uploaded on your media library.

Inserting an photo from your laptop: Upload Files

• First, click on on the button Upload files at the top (if essential).

• Then, click on on at the button Select Files in the center of your display display.

• Pick something image you need out of your device. After you selected your photograph, you may get a pinnacle degree view of pics (media), and your new picture could be decided on.

• Now, on the proper of your display display, insert a short description inside the Title place and the Alt Text difficulty.

These fields are vital for searching for engine advertising and marketing (Search Engine Optimization)

• The final options are the Attachment Display Settings: Alignment: Select the manner you would really like to align your picture.

Your textual content may be aligned underneath your photo.

Link to: What occurs at the same time as a vacationer clicks in your photograph? Choose

Custom URL (to hyperlink to a URL), and Attachment Page (will open the photograph inside your internet website), a Media File (will display exceptional the photo in the browser), or None (not something happens).

Size: Select the scale of your photo because it is able to be proven to your put up or net web page.

Note: You need to resize your pics earlier than you add them because it takes a long time to add huge images.

• Click the Insert into Post button to consist of the photograph: Once you have have been given inserted an picture, that image can also be uploaded into your media library.

Inserting an picture that you already uploaded: Media Gallery

Adding an picture from the media library works pretty loads the identical way as which includes an photo from your device. The tremendous distinction is that you have to select out Media Gallery. However, in case you already brought an photograph, this will already be determined on.

Hyperlinks

A hyperlink is honestly a link that could be a connection with statistics that exists someplace else as an entire record or even a part of it. It can be activated if the reader or client taps or clicks and is used to navigate among net sites and pages.

Using the WYSIWYG editor supplied by manner of the usage of WordPress, placing a hyperlink proper right right into a put up or net internet page is straightforward.

Just have a look at those steps, and you are actual to move.

• First, highlight the textual content you want to expose proper into a hyperlink

• In the menu, click on on on the Link button (Insert or edit link)

A pop up will seem, and following it, there are choices. If you would like to hyperlink to an outside internet web web page:

• Insert the entire URL (which includes "HTTP ://") of the internet web page you selected within the concern ' URL.'

• Type a brief description of what you are approximately to link in your internet internet site on line within the Title vicinity.

• Click "Open link in a present day window/tab" definitely so the web web page will open in a new window/tab.

• Click the Add Link button.

If you would like to link to an internal internet page (that is one internal your internet web website online or weblog) that already exists:

• Select the option underneath the fields that say; Or hyperlink to modern-day content material material.

• When the "Search" vicinity pops up, you could input a part of the grow to be aware about of the submit or page which you are seeking out.

• Choose a placed up or internet internet web page from the listing.

• You should quality click on on; Open link in a brand new window/tab if you select that the put up or web page opens in a very new window or tab, but it isn't a high-quality choice when you have related to an inner web web page.

• Then click on on the upload link button.

How to edit a hyperlink.

• Select the text of which you have already made a link (you do no longer want to pick out the complete textual content, it is best to click on on on on it as speedy as).

• Click at the Link button within the menu (to Insert or edit hyperlink).

• Carry out the crucial changes you need.

• Click at the Update button, after which the modifications is probably stored and performed.

How to take away a link

• Highlight the text of which you have already created a link (you do now not need to pick out the whole text, it's miles excellent to click on on on it as soon as).

• Click the unlink button.

Chapter 7: Let's Communicate About The Appearance Of Your

internet web site online

One of the excellent capabilities of a WordPress internet site is the quick customizable alternatives that it gives you with at the pass; not best has re-growing your website online to suit your taste become much less complicated, however there also are heaps of options to select from at the same time as selecting a format for your internet site.

All way to WordPress topics.

How to choose out the fine issue be counted to suit your net web site

In WordPress, the content cloth of your web web page isn't straight away related to the format of the said net website on line. You can transfer from one problem rely to the opposite without touching the content. If you sense it's time for a alternate of scenery without tampering with all of your content material cloth, all you need to do is installation a ultra-modern topic!

The extraordinary detail is there are pretty a few alternatives reachable, so absolutely there can be some thing for you, and whatever it's far, you have got to show the area through WordPress.

With an innumerable quantity of layouts staring proper at you, how do which one is the outstanding choice for you? How do which gives are incredible on your net site?

With loads to pick out from, you are surrounded on every spot through using are free issues, industrial topics, frameworks, or you can even create your subject from scratch.

One issue that ought to continuously be leading aspect, even though, is the cause of your net web site. When you pick out out a topic, ensure it is usually used for the same concept because it turned into created for.

You can not assume to apply a sports activities difficulty be counted for a style internet web site and anticipate topics to appearance right. When choosing a subject, discover ways to use one immediately or carefully associated with the intention of the net web page.

Free subjects

You can find out pretty a huge sum of loose topics at the internet. In a few instances, unfastened problems are fantastic to find out if you are new to WordPress, or if you have a incredible finances.

But don't worry, a whole lot of those problems are of right extraordinary.

The exceptional place to begin seeking out a free scenario keep in mind is the listing of the most famous unfastened WordPress topics on the legit WordPress net website on-line. Using a unfastened difficulty additionally may be a wonderful stepping stone to growing your subject matter.

Commercial topics

Commercial venture subjects are regularly referred to as Premium subject subjects. In stylish, commercial enterprise issues offer an entire lot more possibilities and even higher aid.

Themeforest and WooThemes are right net websites to check for expert answers. Their problems aren't difficult to apply and cheap. All you want to do is pick out a theme you need, after which there are but pretty some alternatives to customize the problem.

Their fees typically will be inclined to differ, but maximum topics rate amongst $45 and $fifty five.

Another choice is thru a WordPress Framework. This desire is first-class for builders who would like to create their very personal (infant) subject on top of a framework. Two of the maximum well-known frameworks are Thesis and

Genesis.

Create your trouble rely (coding/decreasing)

Taking it upon your self to code your theme is the only maximum honest manner to create a topic be counted range. Creating a subject using WordPress is more trustworthy than one may additionally anticipate. The handiest disadvantage is that it without a doubt takes greater time.

If you're interested in coding your challenge, you have to recall using a WordPress framework like Genesis; this makes it an lousy lot less complicated to create a compelling and solid challenge depend.

Another method that is used lots is reducing. In this example, your subject matter is designed in Photoshop and send it to a slicing organization (you could additionally do this your self in case you are accurate at developing your WordPress problems). The lowering business enterprise agency will then expand a WordPress topic of your Photoshop layout.

Installing a subject rely

There are three primary strategies to feature and installation a topic in WordPress:

• Using FTP

• Uploading a subject thru the WordPress Dashboard

• Choose a loose assignment thru the WordPress Dashboard For most clients, the usage of the WordPress Dashboard may be the very pleasant way.

Using FTP

• First, download your problem in your computer

• Then, upload your project depend to your internet website hosting (the use of FTP) into the folder wp-content fabric and internal it - subjects.

• Log in through the decrease once more end of your WordPress weblog or internet net web page and click on on Appearance and then Themes in the left menu

• You will find your newly added state of affairs depend within the list of to be had subject matters:

• Click the Activate button below the venture remember to spark off it.

• You can head to the of the residence net web page of your weblog or net web page to look the stop result

To upload a topic remember via the WordPress dashboard Note: You might require this feature in case you pick to buy a enterprise subject matter.

• The first step could be to download a subject into your laptop.

• Select Appearance and then Themes.

• Click the Install troubles tab

• Now, the Upload link.

• Then choose out a Zip report for your computer and click on the button Install Now.

• Once the topic has been installed, click on on at the Activate link:

• Then head to the house web page of your net web site online or weblog to peer the modifications.

To pick out a loose topic thru the WordPress dashboard The

first

path

of

motion

could

be

to

pass

to www.WordPress.Org/extend/problem matters/ and search for a subject you need.

• Once once more, make your manner to Themes via Appearance on the navigation tab.

• Click the button that publicizes Install Themes, observed through the Search button.

• In the space furnished, enter the decision of the topic or the writer and click the Search button.

• After your seek give up result seems, comply with the smooth on-show alternatives.

• Click the Install hyperlink beneath the problem you need to install:

• You can see the effects of a subject be counted you in fact were given with the useful resource of clicking the Live Preview button or take a look at with the aid of clicking Apply.

A subject matter gives you manage over your internet internet page's trendy ap pearance,

including fonts, solar shades,

and web page format.

You pick to use a

free issue depend, or you may select to pay for one of the pinnacle the mes. Here, our reputation will in particular be at the subjects you can get for free of charge.

To manipulate your default problems, click on on Appearance then Themes beginning the navigation area interior your dashboard. Select Add New in case you choice for a modern subject matter to be set up. You can be transferred to a thematic listing this is truly free. You can use the Search or the Filters to discover a fashion you would really like to apply. Once the difficulty you sense is right is selected, click the Preview button to view the manner and way it's far furnished for your

index-76_1.Jpg

internet site. If you're glad with your selected end result, press the Install button.

You can regardless of the reality that customize the topic that have become already hooked up with the help of a topic don't forget customizing device in WordPress. Just click at the Appearance section in the menu at the left, select Customize. When you get there, you may modify the arrival of the winning issue matter consistent along with your dreams thru the usage of adjusting the statistics photograph, colorations, menus, the web page identity, and others.

What are the menus and widgets?

After set up, WordPress mechanically offers a menu in your weblog or net site. The gain of that is that you

do not should do a unmarried problem to create a menu. The drawback, however, is that some of the competencies aren't person-pleasant in that particular second in case you would really like to reserve the menu devices or to function a category or an outside link for your menu. Some plugins can treatment this, but it's miles an extended manner less difficult to create a custom menu.

How to create a custom menu

Select Appearance, and then you may moreover click on on Menus within the left menu. Following the on-display activate, next, enter the decision of your new menu and pick out the Create Menu button, and the present day menu will now seem on the right part of your display.

How to attach a custom menu in your issue

This varies with subjects, however commonly, a topic count number can help or extra menus, custom menus. You can pick which menu to apply at whichever location within the Theme Locations difficulty. Just pick out out the menu you would really like to use after which click the Save button.

Add custom links, pages and categories for your menu Add a custom link for your menu

Custom Links can be brought in your menu inside the segment Custom Links; a ll you are required to do is to insert a URL, a menu label after that after which, click on on the Add to Menu button to add the link for your menu.

Add pages for your menu

Pages may be brought for your menu in from the Pages aspect: Choose the web page(s) you would really like to characteristic for your menu and click on on the Add to Menu Link underneath.

Note, if the internet web page you need to insert already exists and isn't always indexed inside the Most Recent tab, look for it within the View All or Search tab.

Add education on your menu

Categories can be delivered on your menu within the Categories element:

First, select out the magnificence or classes that you would like to insert into your menu and click on the Add to Menu button.

index-79_1.Jpg

Note, if the elegance you want to function, exists, and is not listed within the maximum contemporary-day tab, try to test the View All or Search tab.

How to trade the order of the menu gadgets

The order of menu items can without issues be changed by means of the use of hovering along with your cursor over a menu object and dragging into the right location.

How to create a submenu

A menu object also can be set as a sub-object inside the menu, really via dragging a menu object a chunk bit to the right under the parent internet web page.

How to take away a menu object

A menu item may be eliminated through heading to the Menus show, then click on on on the arrow on the proper of a menu item.

Select the Remove Link and click on Save in a while to update your menu.

Widgets

A widget is a small application or extensions which you may area in a region furnished on your weblog or internet net web site; it's also on a column left or right on the internet web page (wherein additionally the menu is placed) or a region at the lowest of the blog or net website online. There is a restrained extensive sort of areas to vicinity widgets is and will be and is predicated upon on the difficulty getting used.

Widgets have severa thrilling potentials. There are widgets to:

• Display all of the pages or categories of a weblog or website

• Fill in some textual content

• Show your cutting-edge tweets from Twitter

• Display business

Widgets come up with the capability to regulate the content material and the format of your internet web page with out difficulty and unexpectedly. Under the Appearance section, you could get proper of access to them whilst you click on at the Dashboard. There, you will be supplied a catalog of widgets to be had. By default, there need to already be a Primary Sidebar, a Footer Widget Area, and a Content Sidebar.

Be sure to take a look at that, however, the quantity of widgets is predicated upon sorely is based upon on which WordPress concern take into account is getting used. If you want to embody a widget, all you need to do is expand the world you would like the widget to be, drag and drop your widget to this area, and then press Save. If you would like to remove a widget, click on the chosen widget and drag it out the widget problem. If you need to region your text right right into a widget, pick out a certain textual content overlay and embed the HTML code.

Chapter 8: What Do I Do With The Ones Things Referred To As

comments?

Beneath every submit, there may be an area for site visitors to move away some remarks for the writer/proprietor/creator/admin. This phase is what makes the posts interactive.

How to control remarks

The Comments segment that exists at the dashboard gives the functionality so that you can approve, edit, respond, direct mail, or trash a commentary from the dashboard, eliminating it from that location sincerely. The comment will awesome seem stay at the net internet website underneath the submit handiest if you have general it.

Users and the jobs they are able to play

WordPress has an in-constructed person management machine this is as a substitute effective. Within it, there are numerous man or woman roles to pick out from.

They deliver your net internet site on line's clients get right of access to to numerous traits for your net website online. The maximum authoritative and influential role is called the admin characteristic. The administrator able to performing any operation. No rules for this position exist, so that you need to be aware about who you deliver this function to. An character with this function can delete your complete internet internet site on line, so make sure you only offer the administrator get proper of access to to humans you believe.

To manage your clients, you want to click on customers at the left menu inside the admin segment. There, you can upload, edit, and delete customers.

You can also regulate their names, touch facts, passwords, and specific info.

You won't want to alter distinct customer's statistics, however you can carry out this each sometimes. The addition of recent customers and redefinition of their permissions may be the maximum out of all of the operations you will be carrying out.

To add a modern-day day client: Click Add New desire. Input the specified information and keep.

• Username (required): Create and offer the username of the modern-day individual.

• E-mail (required): Provide the e-mail address of the state-of-the-art person.

• First Name: Insert the patron's first name.

• Last Name: Insert the consumer's final call.

• Website: Here, you could enter the decision of the consumer's net website.

• Password (times, required): Customize and enter a robust password for your new consumer.

• Send Password: You should most effective use this option in case you need to send the password to the individual.

• Role: Choose a feature on your new character.

After all the fields were stuffed, click on on the Add New User to create the contemporary user.

To exchange user permissions: Within the purchaser vicinity, choose out the patron's name you need to alter. Where it shows feature, choose the best characteristic. Then navigate down and select Update User to replace your modifications.

Here is a short rationalization of each feature a patron can take in interior WordPress.

• Administrator – Has get right of entry to to everything and a few aspect. There is not any limit to his or her obtain interior net web page.

• Editor – Has get right of access to to all pages, posts, commands, feedback, tags, and hyperlinks. They furthermore have the right to create posts and pages.

• Author – They can write, add documents, edit the posts, and post posts of their personal.

• Contributor – This function can't submit or add, however they could write and alter their posts and located up them.

• Follower/Viewer–

They can best test and

comment on pages and posts.

For safety motives, it is recommended that you create debts; one for reinforcing and developing contents, some other with administrative control for configuration, and installations of critical software application concerning the web net website.

Also, ensure your username is not admin; find out a few different as quickly as possible if this is the case because your desire has left you open to hackers.

How to increase the number one person manage

Generally talking, WordPress provided simple consumer control is greater than sufficient. However, in case you experience the need to increase the winning roles, or in case you would really like to create new roles, then you could installation the User Access Manager Plugin.

Chapter 9: The Mysterious Helpers Which Might Be Plugins

Plugins appear to be the real power of WordPress; plugins can be seen as small programs giving you the possibility to boom the functionalities of a fundamental WordPress installation. Most plugins, thankfully, may be downloaded and established free of price.

Today, there are thousands of plugins available, gift for the exceptional motive of growing capability. For every particular characteristic or feature, you would love to feature in your website; an answer lies someplace within the form of a plugin.

How to choose an exquisite plugin

If you're looking for unfastened plugins, it is probably remarkable to leaf through the internet site of WordPress itself. A large indicator of beneficial plugins is the popularity – how many humans are speakme about it, and are their remarks great? So it is a superb idea to find out the list of the maximum popular plugins:

http://WordPress.Org/boom/plugins/browse/famous/

Commercial plugins

Apart from free plugins, there are also commercial plugins. If you're looking for commercial enterprise plugins, a brilliant spot to find out them may be Codecanyon.Internet. Several scripts for developers can be determined on this internet web site on-line, but furthermore clean to apply.

How to install a plugin

Search for the plugin of your choice and set up it thru the again prevent, as maximum of the plugins can be established thru the WordPress Dashboard:

• Click Plugins and then choose out Add New inside the left menu

• On top of this net web page, click on on at the Search hyperlink

• In the quest discipline, input (part of) the call of the plugin and click on at the Search Plugins button

• Soon, you could gather a listing of search effects, and as speedy as you have were given placed the plugin in that you had been looking for in the are searching for for consequences list, click on on the Install Now hyperlink. You receives a pop up for confirmation. Click the OK button.

• After the plugin has been established successfully, click on the Activate plugin hyperlink.

• Do no longer neglect about to configure the plugin.

How to configure a plugin

Before a plugin may be used, it wishes to be configured first; this suggests some settings need to be set; this varies from plugin to plugin, as a few plugins have some settings, and a few unique plugins have masses more settings.

Do your incredible to undergo all the settings and make suitable adjustments.

How to add and set up a plugin via the decrease lower back give up

Some plugins can best be right away downloaded on your tool from the writer's (author's) internet website. Most of those instances are regarding commercial enterprise plugins. Luckily WordPress has a integrated function to upload and installation downloaded plugins.

• Start via choosing Plugins and then Add New inside the left menu.

• Click the Upload link:

• Select a ZIP-file containing the plugin in your computer and click on at the Install button.

- After the plugin has been installation successfully, click on the Activate now Link to release it.

- Don't neglect approximately to configure the plugin.

Chapter 10: Safety First

Security is a severe trouble. These days, it looks as if the slightest errors can also want to reason disastrous outcomes, sooner or later of which plenty of loss could be suffered.

You need to take it upon yourself to enforce protection measures to shield your internet internet site or weblog from volatile events.

The following pointers will no longer assure that you will be genuinely loose from malicious assaults, but it will make you a tough target.

Basic safety protocols that make certain your safety WordPress safety includes many things: it's miles about choosing the right character call, composing a strong password, ensuring to update WordPress and all of the plugins to their current

versions. It does now not seem like a few trouble specific, but they do help!

Choosing the proper admin client name

While putting in, you may ought to pick out a client name for the administrator account of your weblog or net net web page. You shouldn't select an clean to guess user call, like admin or perhaps administrator; because of the fact this is one of the topics hackers attempt first!

Make a 2nd person account for updating the content material cloth This is a mistake made through some of bloggers; they blog with their administrator consumer. Do not try this! Make use of an editor for this. Just if a hacker by using way of a few approach manages to retrieve the password of the character you which you are the use of to weblog, they may log in as an editor and can trade or delete the content cloth fabric, however they may now not be capable of exchange or delete your weblog or internet site.

Picking a sturdy password

Do now not pick out an clean password to have some trouble clean so that you will no longer overlook it. Instead, customise a strong

103

password containing; letters (differing instances), numbers,

and precise characters. Try not to pick out a short password for the sake of simplicity.

Change the table prefix

While you've got been installing, WordPress offers you a choice to trade the prefix of your database tables. By default, this is; WP_. If this is accomplished, you may make it very hard for hackers to bet your desk names.

Keep WordPress and all its plugins updated to the contemporary day versions

This is an easy step, but furthermore a very vital step. When a new version of WordPress is released, it does no longer nice add new capabilities, however it additionally resolves bugs and patches protection issues. That is why it is vital always to have the modern day model of WordPress, further to the plugins.

Make backups

By backing up your WordPress internet web page, you're making sure that every one of your facts is saved secure in an opportunity area.

Just in case a few issue goes wrong together together together with your WordPress internet net site, a backup is an splendid way to make sure that each one of your files can be restored to their particular circumstance.

Updates and manage

WordPress commonly handles small updates itself, so you do now not usually should worry about it. The big ones will continuously provide you with the selection to update at your preferred time. Meanwhile, you can research the features of the trendy update or positioned your internet site online on upkeep mode.

There are three crucial stuff you have to often update on your WordPress internet web page; WordPress itself, troubles, and plugins.

You can update your internet internet site on-line from the Update section in the navigation bar.

Your entire WordPress website online want to be continuously updated; this is vital because of the truth whilst a subject or a plugin is updated, new functionalities and worm fixes may be made to be had.

It is likewise an crucial part of maintaining a WordPress net internet site strong and speedy.

Chapter 11: Easy Tricks For Great Searching For Engine Advertising

If that's what you are looking beforehand to from this e-book, you will in all likelihood need to take a second to take a look at the fact of present day search engine optimization. Search engines like Google had been often enhancing their algorithms. While they're far from ideal, it is more hard to fool them in recent times. The fact is, if you want to rank properly in the engines like google — you're better off making valuable webpages, with content fabric that humans in truth need to view. Once you are able to make, or buy, appropriate content material material, you could enforce the hunt engine marketing strategies (which aren't tips) in the ones pages.

Make Content for Humans

It is crucial to recall which are not sincerely writing content material for the hunt engine crawlers. If you begin to write for algorithms, you may become failing in the long run. Little "recommendations" that art work properly for rating highly unhelpful content cloth inside the inside the meantime, might probable result in your area being punished inside the destiny.

For instance, Google is constantly going for walks to enhance their are seeking for engine's effectiveness at connecting humans with suitable and beneficial content material.

People are folks who will in the end decide how a achievement your internet website online is, due to the reality you can't assume any reasonably-priced tricks to preserve jogging for all time. People also want to percentage subjects that they select, and you could get plenty greater website on-line site visitors with a brilliant internet website online, than you can with trickery.

Make content material for human beings first, and try to use right, lengthy-lasting seek engine advertising and marketing techniques once you've performed that.

Advanced Keyword Research

The first difficulty most people probably study, once they begin to dive into the world of seo, is the time period "key-word". If you're analyzing this financial catastrophe on superior key-word research, it's solid to count on that you don't need an evidence of the basics.

Top Keyword Research Tools

When you're looking for rather treasured key terms, a simple key-phrase research device isn't always going to get the project accomplished. Those are extraordinary for finding out the extent stages of key terms, relative to others. However, you want to transport deeper than that, and the following tools will assist.

Google's key-word tool. This is good for finding out the common searches for a key-word, in quantity.

MSN's Adcenter key-word device. This shows unique counts, and it need to offer you with quite dependable facts.

Wordtracker's keyword tool. The Wordtracker tool isn't quite as accurate because the Google or MSN device. It remains suitable for buying a relative extent estimation.

You must no longer be using without a doubt one approach for finding key-word records, in case you need to transport into a sophisticated level of key-word studies.

See What's Trending

Now which you have a few first-rate assets for are seeking volume, and relative amount, it's time to look at tendencies. Do you recognise at the same time as queries in your key phrases are at their peaks? Perhaps you've got visible a drop-off inside the effectiveness of a number of your key terms, however you're no longer positive at the same time as this commenced out to expose up. You need some wonderful equipment for locating out at the same time as your key phrases are acting nicely, or failing.

• Google Trends for Keywords

• MSN AdCenter Labs: Keyword Forecast Tool

You will possibly be surprised to find out what key phrases are trending the most. This is likewise going to provide you a few perception into what's causing your personal key phrases to carry out the way they do.

Create Records

Create a spreadsheet of the key phrases that seem to be well-known, and embody any statistics that your tool offer you with.

It is critical to have the information, however ultimately, you clearly pleasant want to pick out one over the opportunity. Even the best studies tools can be manner off with their numbers, but they may have the capability to show you the rate of a key-phrase, relative others. Don't get too hung up on the figures, due to the fact they may be frequently defective.

Long-Tail and Short-Tail Keywords

A "short-tale" key-phrase is specially brief, and may even incorporate sincerely one word. In evaluation, a "prolonged-tail" key-phrase is usually at least three phrases prolonged, or greater. There is fee in both forms of key-phrase lengths. However, you have to observe that it's miles almost always more hard to rank well with a short-tail key-word, because of the reality opposition for those key terms may be an awful lot greater tough. If you don't do not forget that, definitely test out the data on a key-phrase like "video video games", after which evaluate that with "cool free own family video games", or some special prolonged-tail key-word.

Chapter 12: Keyword Analysis

Now which you have an superb concept of the keywords which you would like to intention, it's time to analyze them. This can come to be a little trickier, as you may want to appearance more closely at the numbers, and growth your research into a few new regions. It can be especially traumatic in case you research that none of your chosen key phrases are well really worth pursuing. Of direction, that's why now not each person is an search engine optimization hold close. If you want to reap this commercial enterprise, you want to be willing to make mistakes.

The uncooked numbers don't simply suggest loads, with out placing them into attitude. That approach comparing them to different keywords, and additionally to your competition. You can also moreover discover a key-phrase that does thoroughly, but it's worthless to you if there are too many different domains the usage of that time period.

Find Your Competition

The first step of analyzing your key phrases is to find out who is doing nicely using them. You can start with the useful resource of appearing a easy are trying to find engine question, to show the top-rating domain names on your key phrases. It lets in to have an search engine advertising and marketing plugin set up for your internet browser, and there are various available for Chrome and Firefox.

You need to examine the Google internet internet page rank (GPR) of the competing domains, similarly to web internet web page ranks from unique engines like google like google and yahoo like google that you have available to you. Another step is finding the amount of links which can be directed to the ones domains, similarly to the whole variety of domain names which might be pointing links within the route of your competition. Not that trendy links and amount of linking domain names are separate portions of facts.

Is the Competition Too Tough?

This is a relative query; in case your private location ranks well in the aforementioned areas, you might be capable of tackle a few pretty heavy opposition. For the purpose of this ebook, let's anticipate that you are trying to decorate the seo of a fairly non-aggressive location. Here is how your figures have an impact on your opportunities of doing well with a particular keyword:

Page rank. This is a popular variety that tells you the way specific a looking for engine thinks that domain is. They are much more likely to list URLs from this location in advance than people with weaker rankings.

Links. If a particular area has loads of hyperlinks, a looking for engine will assume it's well-known and properly-regarded inside the on-line network. This technique that it is going to be more difficult to compete with.

The key to locating wonderful key phrases is choosing the ones which can be well-known and precious, but nevertheless have quite clean competition.

WordPress Optimization

WordPress is an outstanding content material material material manage device, because it lets in people to create and function expert net net web sites, without the want for an excessive amount of technical records. This leads many humans to believe that search engine advertising and advertising and marketing in WordPress isn't always sensible. While this platform does take lots of the trouble out of handling your seo, it is crucial which you understand the way to provide your web sites the enhance they need to rank nicely.

Focusing On Your "Keyphrase"

If you are not that specialize in a selected brand name, you need to select a keyphrase that your net internet site will awareness on. Many hyperlinks which you get hold of for your location will point in your homepage.

You can make use of this through leveraging inbound hyperlinks, so your keyphrase relates for your homepage. If you pick out to consciousness on a keyphrase that relates in your whole website, you could clearly find out a few issue non-competitive.

Use an XML Sitemap

What is the primary motive that you want to use an XML sitemap to your net net site? Google says that doing so will assist them to well index every web page on your region. If you have got were given end up search engine advertising and marketing advice right now from the top seek engine within the global — you need to take it. If you have got have been given simply created a contemporary day internet internet page, this need to be one of the first steps that you take to create satisfactory seo.

Sitemaps also are proper for imparting extra statistics approximately your region, in addition to helping to growth the effectiveness of your meta records. The call

"XML sitemap" sounds complex, and that probably scares some of humans away. However, you can use Google's XML sitemaps tool to create one, and there may be moreover a terrific seek engine advertising plugin known as WordPress are seeking for engine marketing by using manner of Yoast. This latter device can take pretty a few the hassle out of optimizing your WordPress net net web page.

Canonicalization

This concept might seem hard, however it's actually quite easy. There are severa techniques that someone ought to write your internet site's URL into a web browser. That manner that there are certainly one of a type URLs for search engines like google and yahoo to index. If you would like to awareness this indexing, you want to permit the search engines like google apprehend which URL to list.

For instance, Google would possibly see which you have www.Yoursite.Com, but there may be also yoursite.Com, and www.Yoursite.Com/index.Html.

You might not even be aware that those unique kinds of the same location exist. They all thing on your homepage, however Google isn't going to cope with them because of the truth the equal URL. You have to inform WordPress which URL to use and, by way of way of using Webmaster Tools, inform Google your selected approach of indexing your place.

How to Use Permalinks

When you post content material, your URLs are known as "permalinks". Since they are surely the hyperlinks the numerous rest of the Internet, and the pages for your internet site online, they're of excessive significance.

Why Optimize Permalinks?

The default URLs to your pages could probably look like a jumbled bunch of letters, numbers, and symbols, following your region call. You can alternate those, without a doubt so your permalinks display the decision of the precise section of your website, and then a legible name. Use key terms that both describe the content material of the net page, and are in step with your seo goals. People not often in reality write down URLs by using manner of hand anymore, so it's exquisite in case your URLs are at the longer factor.

While you can change your permalinks any time you need, it'll probably bring about a drop in website visitors for your internet web page. Your pages may be re-indexed through the years, but it is nevertheless a better concept to select permalinks that you are glad with, proper from the start.

CMS Permalinks

Content control structures, together with WordPress, make the tool of customizing your permalinks quite easy. You can installation your chosen publishing tool to automatically layout your URLs in a certain manner. If you would like to alter any precise one, that is furthermore smooth to do.

How to Format Your Permalinks

Some human beings choose out to include some part of the date of book, including the three hundred and sixty five days and month, as part of their permalinks. The choice is yours, but you need to be conscious that the important thing terms in your permalinks do have an effect on the tremendous of your search engine optimization.

Usually, with none customization, computerized or otherwise, the shape of your permalinks will no longer appearance very customer-splendid.

For instance, they'll appearance a few issue like this: www.Yourwebsite.Com/?Page_id=4532.

You can see how it would be heaps extra most suitable to have permalinks that look more like this: www.Yourwebsite.Com/my-exceptional-weblog-put up.

Despite what you could pay attention some vicinity else, Google is able to indexing URLs with question strings. However, they have got sincerely stated that more patron-first-rate established permalinks are less complex for their crawlers to index.

How to Use Tags Correctly

There look like countless plugins and approaches for developing your search engine advertising with tags, but right here are the most essential topics which you ought to research.

Title Tags

Typically, people have their net internet web page's call because the call tag for their pages. You are maximum in all likelihood jogging to rank the decision of your internet web page already, so why do you need to embody it on your name tag? Instead, you should select each exclusive key-word which you would like to rank nicely for, and use that as your name tag.

There are numerous critiques about the way to make the best name tags. A common exercise is to apply your number one key-phrase, accompanied thru your secondary key-phrase. After using the ones phrases or phrases, you may area the call of your internet web page or logo.

Remember that serps like google and yahoo will great show a nice sort of characters out of your pick out out tags. For this reason, you need to try and make your titles among 50 to 60 characters, or heaps a lot much less. You could make your titles longer, however make certain that your maximum essential keywords are right on the the front.

Meta Tags

Meta records is most with out problems defined as being records that is about statistics. Your meta tags are speculated to assist serps like google properly categorize your webpages. Generally, human beings do no longer positioned a whole lot benefit within the usage of meta tags. In the past, they were taken into consideration extraordinarily critical for proper SEO. In fact, many site owners have been able to get wonderful rankings, for domain names that contained little-to-no beneficial content cloth, via tricking these primitive algorithms. That have become additionally one of the motives for the search engines like google and yahoo improving their indexing systems.

These days, Search engines like Google use a protracted manner more advanced algorithms, simply so they do now not want to depend upon meta tags. However, you can alternate the ones to provide your self an introduced search engine optimization enhance. Keep in mind that meta tags don't definitely have an effect on are looking for effects masses any more, inside the occasion that they do in any respect. Despite this, it's despite the fact that a terrific idea to preserve the exercise of optimizing your meta tags. You by no means understand even as Google's algorithms will alternate, or those of other search engines like google and yahoo like google.

Chapter 13: How To Structure Your First Paragraphs

Your first paragraph is an essential detail of any a fulfillment search engine optimization methods. While that is real, earlier than you worry approximately structuring your text for proper are searching for engine advertising and advertising, you need to make certain that your traffic will need to have a look at it. As extended as you are doing this, you may float onto the ones useful tips.

Keyword Placement

A not unusual seo technique is to apply your number one key-phrase as soon as in the first paragraph of your content material cloth material. Some people claim that doing this within the first sentence is maximum useful, however that desire is yours. You shouldn't allow any character "rule" to dominate all of your content material fabric. It is also an terrific idea to encompass plenty of possibility key phrases that relate in your primary key-word.

First Paragraph Structure

There must be three (or perhaps four) sentences to your first paragraph. You should also ask a question, or make a announcement approximately what people can anticipate to have a look at within the rest of the net internet page's content fabric. Whatever you do, make certain to keep away from using huge blocks of textual content. Allow hundreds of white place, and by no means have a very long first paragraph. Think of it as the first affect that you get to make on site visitors. If you mess this up, you would possibly in no manner begin to draw extra site visitors.

Restate the Promise Your Title Gave

It's critical that your content material cloth offers customers the statistics that they've been promised through your emerge as aware about. If you operate interest-grabbing headings that aren't addressed on your content material cloth — and ideally inside the first paragraph — human beings can be possibly to transport a few different area for what they want. In addition, besides you can maintain people's interest along side your first paragraph, you could lose the accept as authentic with of your site visitors.

Why Content Is As Important as Structure

How is all this critical to search engine advertising and advertising? If humans do no longer live to your pages for prolonged, or you have were given a excessive rate of customers leaving your vicinity speedy, it could definitely hurt how lots Google values your region famous.

How to Structure Your Last Paragraph

As with the number one paragraph, many search engine optimization specialists undergo in mind the very last paragraph to be very critical.

Your crucial key-phrase ought to be present inside the very last paragraph of your content fabric cloth, and you may choose to location it in the final sentence.

What Are Last Paragraphs Good For?

Think of your very last paragraph as a end. You don't want to use a "Conclusion" sub-heading, but it ought to be obvious that your content material cloth is coming to an prevent. Try to restate how your content material material has been beneficial, and create a "call to motion", that publications human beings toward the issue that you need from them. This can also have the added gain of enhancing your income, or whatever else you're hoping to build up collectively along with your net web site.

Keyword Density Tips

Since using key terms can growth your seo, it would seem as although getting a top score ought to be easy. Often, novices assume that it is a top notch idea to really stuff their content material with precious key phrases. After all, Google is fantastic to provide your webpages precedence, if you use the right key phrases, right? That form of thinking will not help you inside the slightest, so it's exceptional to put off it out of your planning proper away.

Forget the Past

Back in the early days, whilst search engines like google and yahoo first started out out to make use of algorithms for list internet web sites, subjects were less complicated for search engine optimization specialists. The problem changed into, that humans may want to truely break out with in reality stuffing their websites with keywords. Many human beings might even disguise them throughout their pages, truly so customers couldn't see them. The are trying to find engine crawlers need to choose out out these up, but. This bring about plenty of lousy net websites rating fantastically inside the search engines like google like google like google and yahoo, at the equal time as some extraordinary net web sites in truth could not get a smash.

Whatever you keep in mind the newer, smarter, algorithms that search engines like google are the usage of, they have got clearly advanced the tremendous of internet net websites that humans can without issue find.

Perfecting Keyword Density

Instead of obsessing about key-word density, and searching out the exceptional method for key-word use, make precise content material material cloth. Once you have got this, you want to ensure that your key-phrase density is handiest 1% to five%. Yes, there's hundreds of room for personal preference interior the ones numbers. That's due to the fact the reality is, no character is privy to at the same time as are searching for engine algorithms would possibly change all once more, and punish a positive degree of keyword density. It's maximum stable to keep your key-word use to a minimum, while still focusing on them truely sufficient to live aggressive.

For example, when you have 500 phrases of content material material fabric on a page, and you use a specific key-phrase 10 times, you will have a key-word density of %. Some users may also discover that that is already too regularly to replicate the same key-phrase or word, so be cautious. Good search engine advertising and marketing would possibly backfire, if you alienate your site site visitors.

Chapter 14: How To Optimize Your Images

You might also anticipate that seek engine advertising is all about the use of the textual content to your web page, and to your meta data, properly. However, the manner that you use pictures in your location can increase your traffic via the use of a large amount. This is why it's miles essential to learn how to properly optimize your pix for awesome seo.

Crawlers and Images

Humans can take a look at an photograph, and rapid recognize what it's far about. That might be wonderful for humans, but search engine crawlers aren't present day sufficient (but) to actually understand the content material fabric fabric of pics. You want to nicely format your image-associated textual content, in order that the crawlers can index all the content material material of your website properly, collectively together with your pics.

Image Alt Text

This is basically text that may be used by search engines like google like google and yahoo, with a view to apprehend what a selected picture is. Your pics have a document name, and it's up to you to pick out what this could be.

For instance, you'll probably truly use a machine of dates or numbers, like: image2_2016.Jpg, and that is flawlessly right. It might be greater available in the future, in case you label your pics with a few aspect extra customer-great, like: summer_sunrise_5_2016.Jpg. However, that lets in you to advantage you the maximum, and make managing your documents plenty less tough in the future.

As to your alt textual content, you need to use your focus key-phrase for that net internet web page. If you have got had been given written a bit of writing approximately summer time, and the summer season dawn image from the preceding instance is featured, you could make your alt text some factor like: Beautiful Summer Sunrise. This will inform the hunt engine crawlers what the image is, and allow them to index your content fabric nicely.

Plugin Settings

The chances are that you'll use plugins for your internet site. These are quantities of software software program which might be made for use with numerous content material material manage systems and outstanding software program software. Think of them as little extensions, which add more functionality to what you are already using.

Wordpress and Yoast's SEO plugin

As WordPress is one of the most widely used content management systems within the global, it is able to pay to grow to be acquainted with the sort of plugins which may be to be had for it. Yoast's WordPress seo plugin is probably one of the first rate plugins that you may installation for assisting at the side of your seo. While you can't expect plugins to do all the give you the results you want, they do take masses of problem from your internet site responsibilities.

Be Careful Changing Settings

Before you start messing with any settings, make sure which you understand what your adjustments should affect. The last component you want to do is destroy some thing interior your internet site.

Whatever search engine optimization plugin you pick out, it want to have at the least the following number one capabilities:

•   Permalink customization that can be changed within the destiny.

- Optimized pick out out and heading introduction.

- Search engine description optimization.

- Image alt text optimization.

- Simple XML sitemap introduction.

- Breadcrumbs.

Your plugin want to furthermore let you know how correct your seek engine marketing and advertising and marketing is for each of your pages, and what you may do to restoration any mistakes.

Avoid Bad Plugins

While you could discover a big variety of various plugins, and you can possibly be tempted to put in many of them — be cautious together together with your choice of plugins. Using too many is an easy manner to smash your internet site's pace. In addition to that, a few plugins do no longer come from reliable property.

How to Use Categories to Improve Your On-Page seo

You might probable consider your training as a simple way to arrange and archive all the pages in your net web page. While they do fulfil this want, you can additionally use your classes to boom your seek engine marketing effectiveness.

Use Unique Text

As with all website introduction, you need to be targeted on developing specific content cloth — for every new internet page which you make. This can turn out to be a bit tough in terms of creating beauty pages. It is all too smooth to absolutely use critical, "boilerplate" content material for each of those pages. They are actually going to list everything internal a specific elegance, regardless of the whole thing, so people frequently neglect approximately about their significance.

Search engines are able to spotting duplicated content material cloth, and they will even punish you with poorer ratings, in case your page includes some of repeated content fabric. Even if every of your class pages is essentially giving the equal statistics, approximately one-of-a-type lessons, you have to make the effort to rewrite them, just so they appear precise. Better still, you may think about some useful content material fabric to encompass that relates to what people can discover internal that segment of your internet web page.

This kind of element might appear like a waste of time to many webmasters. However, those are the types of techniques that in reality dedicated seo masters make use of. If you need to acquire success, you have to be inclined to do even the smallest aspect, to provide your self an advantage over the opposition.

More than Lists

Many of your mid-tier class pages are probably little more than lists of the pages they hyperlink to. However, in case you want to enhance your are seeking engine advertising, you need to encompass at the least a hundred to 100 fifty terms of precise content cloth.

How to Analyze Your On-Page are trying to find engine advertising for FREE and Fix Errors Fast

You may take a look at every single search engine marketing tip that exists, in addition to a way to nicely put in force your knowledge. However, as you grow to be greater involved in seo, and start to create greater net web sites — you may eventually need a assisting hand. That is in which a few remarkable search engine advertising and marketing tool will become your fantastic pals.

Staying Up-to-Date

One of the most important traumatic situations going thru seek engine advertising and marketing professionals is the manner that the Internet is continuously converting. A device this is noticeably beneficial today, may want to likely come to be all but worthless in every week's time. That is why you should usually ensure that your records is cutting-edge, and which you never turn out to be complacent together together with your preference of system.

Here is a listing of effective, well-known, and modern search engine optimization gadget that you can use to research your internet web sites:

Ahrefs. If you want to research your hyperlinks, you need to apply a consultant device. Ahrefs supply in-depth evaluations for any precise domain which you want to observe.

Majestic. This is a quite well-known tool for pretty a few seo specialists. It is considered very accurate and reliable.

SEMrush. This is a superb device in case you would like to investigate your competition. If Google's analytics tool received't assist you to get right of entry to the rank for a domain, this is the tool which you need at your disposal.

BuzzSumo. This is extremely good for searching at the seo rate of your content material material. It can figure out what number of stocks your content material material cloth has gotten on websites like Facebook and Twitter, or perhaps allow you to examine your competition.

Once you have positioned in which you want to enhance your net web sites, you need to do some thing to restore your mistakes as rapid as viable.

Proven Off-Page Optimization Tactics

While the statistics on this book has been in big part approximately assisting you decorate the on-internet page search engine advertising and advertising of your webpages, you have to do not forget your off-net web page are trying to find engine advertising and marketing as properly.

What Is Off-Page are seeking engine advertising?

Off-net net page search engine advertising and marketing absolutely refers to a few aspect which you are capable of do away from your internet site, which can help you to rank better with the engines like google like google like google and yahoo. This includes things like submitting articles, the usage of social networks, interacting on forums, and writing visitor posts on notable people's blogs.

While off-page search engine advertising techniques aren't all about manipulating the search engines like google like google, or providing you with a direct, statistical beautify — they'll be exceedingly critical, and even important, to the success of your different seek engine marketing and advertising strategies.

Guest Posts

If you need to set yourself up as an professional parent, writing a guest placed up for some different net web site is a wonderful concept. Find a person who goals you to share your statistics with their own enthusiasts. This is, of route, a extraordinary way to get a few nicely links flowing on your private net site. Don't just reflect onconsideration on it as some smooth hyperlinks despite the truth that. Write visitor posts which may be particular and treasured, so you will become nicely-reputable through different website owners, similarly to their readers.

When humans see that your opinion is legitimate with the beneficial aid of different authority figures, it will set you up as an authority determine too.

Blogging

Since you are already developing particular content material, how about developing a blog that relates in your internet website online? You ought to make a weblog more non-public than a website, or even upload some posts approximately your private existence. This will make you seem more approachable to your fans. It is likewise a terrific way to generate your personal hyperlinks, among your internet website online and your blog.

Social Networks

If you don't realise what social networks are, you'll probably need to do a little catching up. Sites like Facebook, Twitter, Google+, and LinkedIn have become more famous with the useful aid of the day. It is easy to create a profile for yourself on one (or many) of these net websites. You may additionally even create a profile for your website or corporation.

Once you are related, you'll see how effective social media without a doubt is. It is a incredible manner to create buzz approximately your non-public content material material fabric, and to have interaction with human beings in the network, who're interested by the location of interest of your net internet site on line.

Chapter 15: Social Bookmarking

Since you need to be using social community net websites, you can take advantage of social bookmarking. This is the act of submitting links to your very private pages on social bookmark net web sites, together with Digg, Reddit, StumbleUpon, Delicious, and so on. These internet websites aren't masses approximately adding pals and posting about your lifestyles. They are for bookmarking (sharing hyperlinks), after which posting remarks approximately the bookmarks which might be posted.

It in reality doesn't take a good buy try and percent all your posts in the perfect regions of the famous social bookmarking websites. As an added bonus, humans expect to look plenty of links with out a remarks, so there's an lousy lot much less hazard that they will bear in mind you as a spammer.

You can start a few quite in-intensity conversations with people on social bookmarking web sites. Sites like Reddit are continuously updated, so that they have an inclination to get a whole lot of hobby from are looking for engine's crawlers.

Forum and Blog Marketing

Blogs and forums are a exceptional vicinity for people to submit links to their personal websites and products. However, if that is all you do, you aren't any greater than a spammer. Start good sized conversations with human beings, and attempt to put a few thing useful to your posts.

If you be aware that a person has requested a query, or they are searching out assist from a fellow client — that may be a extraordinary opportunity that allows you to add in your photograph as an expert determine.

When posting everywhere at the Internet, you want to normally recall to be courteous and polite. Even if a person attempts to start a combat with you, clearly supply a nice response, and avoid getting twisted up in any arguments.

Search Engine Submission

This is a topic of dialogue among SEO experts. Some humans will assist you to know that you must in no way placed up your internet website online to the search engines like google and yahoo like google. They will in the long run index your pages, so there's no absolute want to post your internet web site. The selection honestly is yours, due to the truth you could in no way get a particular solution from the search engine advertising and marketing network.

Submitting your internet web site can growth the rate at which your internet net web page is listed. It may even provide you with an opportunity to help decide which beauty your internet web website is placed within.

How to Boost Your Rankings with RSS Feeds

If you're analyzing these advanced search engine advertising and advertising and marketing pointers, it's assumed which you apprehend the fundamentals of RSS feeds.

However, you could need to apprehend exactly how their use may possibly affect your are searching for engine ratings.

When Google changed their algorithms to "Hummingbird" in 2013, they began out to popularity greater closely on penalizing duplicated or un-treasured content. While putting your content on an RSS feed will technically be duplicating your pages, search engines like google like google and yahoo must now not penalize you for this.

RSS feeds are not honestly indexed with the aid of Google's crawlers. Instead, they will first-class stumble upon the XML codes that have been used to make the RSS feed. This might likely make it appear as though making an RSS feed could not probable assist your search engine optimization. You need to don't forget that obtaining proper search engine optimization is ready greater than simply building up your facts inside the most obvious methods.

Why RSS Feeds Are Good for seek engine advertising

If you can get humans to sign up for your RSS feed, there may be a chance that they may end up treasured enthusiasts. In addition, you may benefit site visitors for your net website online from your RSS posts. Many humans choose to encompass simply an excerpt in their posts of their RSS feeds. If customers want to examine the relaxation of your content material, they will then want to go to your internet internet site. Either way, search engines like google and yahoo like google will see that humans are spending time for your region, and if you need to certainly help your seo.

You can think about RSS feeds as a shape of seo this is in strategies on-website and rancid-net web site. Since humans are technically getting access to your area whilst analyzing your RSS posts, they're for your net net page. However, for the purpose that they'll be having access to feeds that can not be indexed with the aid of search engines like google and yahoo like google and yahoo, they're now not considered genuinely in your internet site. That would in all likelihood seem complicated, however this is advanced search engine optimization.

It's Open for Debate

Google will no longer simply announce how RSS feeds affect search engine optimization. The fantastic issue to do is use your feed to build up a treasured base of clients. It is likewise advocated which you consist of latest content material cloth on your feeds. Don't use them as a manner to rehash your vintage pages, because that is in reality now not going to assist your seek engine advertising and marketing.

Once your RSS feeds begin to get antique, it's a superb concept to do away with them. If your internet website online covers a large sort of various topics, it might be a remarkable idea to create a couple of feeds. People don't join in RSS feeds to look through a bunch of posts, just to discover what pursuits them. They anticipate content fabric that is custom designed for area of interest audiences.

How to Piggyback Authority Websites to Rank for Competitive Keyword Phrases

If your internet web page online remains quite new, or you advocate to make one inside the future, you need to assume it to take the time to rank well in your number one key phrases. This is a subject that is despite the fact that underneath debate, however many accept as true with that Google prefers domain names which have been spherical for longer. It stands to reason that they might supply priority to older domains, due to the fact those are people who generally have the most useful content material fabric material.

How Can You Use Big Websites to Help Your seo?

If you would like to discover ways to take benefit of the web web page scores of modern net web sites, there may be a easy machine which you want to observe:

•	You need to make a listing of internet sites to your location of interest that appear to be authority internet web sites. This will take a few honest studies, and excessive-ranking internet net web sites are not constantly to most obvious ones.

•	Once you recognize what web sites you would love to "piggyback" on, it's time to determine out what key phrases you'll goal for. Find all of the competitive key terms which you need to use, and make certain they relate on your focused internet web sites.

•	Now all you need to do is create some tremendous content material, including your name for motion and links for your webpages. After this, located up your content fabric fabric on well-known internet web sites, consisting of YouTube, Google+ (it's a commonplace accept as true with that Google favors their own net internet web sites)

Dailymotion, Metacafe, Facebook, Twitter, LinkedIn, DocStoc, Scribd, and so forth.

•   Make certain which you encompass hyperlinks again to your very very personal internet internet site on-line, and don't percentage a few element that is unsolicited mail-like. People must need to have a observe hyperlinks to your internet internet page, from the larger websites, due to the fact they positioned fee in what you shared — not because of the fact you tricked them.

Chapter 16: What Is Wordpress?

The concept of no longer having to interact with plenty of activities on the manner to create and manipulate your private blog or website is the center charge of what WordPress stands for and why it have become created.

So, what genuinely is WordPress? It is an

open supply content fabric manipulate tool (CMS) and website builder. It makes it clean for all people to create and manipulate their non-public blog and net site while not having any in advance expertise or experience as a web developer (Price, 2021).

WordPress is loose to use, and the nice costs you may come upon are month-to-month or annual (it's miles higher to pick out out the as quickly as a year desire, which in the long run appears to be less expensive than a monthly subscription) charges for hosting your internet internet site. The open supply software application lets in one to test the code of the platform and write their private code to make subjects or different plugins. The plugins all variety in nature and make the net internet page extra user-pleasant, as the ones cater to the awesome goals of diverse customers, be them humans or groups—the platform is open to all.

It is and has been the maximum famous and extensively used CMS for net website constructing and running a blog. In reality, more than 40% of all websites presently on-line were constructed and maintained the use of WordPress software (Price,2021).

For us to better understand its reputation and usability, we need to take a adventure lower back in time to its improvement and inception on the market.

Brief History

On the twenty 1/3 of May, 2003, Matt Mullenweg and Mike Little made the very first model of WordPress available to the general public.

It modified into evolved off every different strolling a blog software program, b2/cafelog, that have come to be discontinued in December 2002 with the aid of the use of the use of its French developer, Michel Valdrighi. The internet site have been used to create blogs thru many, but Valdrighi stopped taking walks on developing the internet internet site on line similarly, and because of this it became now not operational (Cladwell, 2019).

Bloggers have been left with out a platform to paintings from, and this inspired Mullenweg and Little—who had been customers of Valdrighi's platform—to create their personal platform. Mullenweg and Little used the b2/cafelog software software, making changes to it so you can create the WordPress platform. Essentially, they stored all the components that labored and introduced functions like a ultra-modern admin interface with templates that had been compliant with XHTML 1.1.

In 2004, model 1.2 of WordPress have end up brought. The new version came with the only essential characteristic that makes WordPress what it is nowadays, and that is the architecture plugin advanced with the beneficial aid of Ryan Boren. This is what permits clients and developers to put in writing down their private plugins and percent them on WordPress for all to use.

WordPress become now formally an open deliver platform, and this become achieved via acquiring the GNU General Purpose License (GPL). This assured that the platform might be free for every purchaser to pass on software software software/code that can be used by the following person, giving them the freedom to run this machine and make any changes to it within the occasion that they so wished (Cladwell, 2019).

During the equal 3 hundred and sixty 5 days, Moveable Type, who have been the marketplace leaders in the going for walks a blog device business business enterprise, decided that could fee them their role and increase each WordPress' following and consumer base. Moveable Type delivered licensing phrases that masses of its customers had been not too thrilled approximately, and they made the skip to WordPress, which furnished itself because the maximum suitable opportunity inside the taking walks a blog company. More clients at the platform intended more thoughts and extra developers to edit the software program code, similarly to to feature plugins.

Two of the most full-size dates in WordPress' records are March 1st, 2006, on the equal time as Mullenweg filed to trademark WordPress and the WordPress emblem underneath Automatic, a corporation he co-based, and June of 2010, while the ownership of WordPress have become transferred from Automatic to the WordPress Foundation. The nonprofit basis emerge as based by using the use of Mullenweg just so WordPress may also need to not be relying on one individual or commercial enterprise employer, consequently fending off the identical destiny as Valdrighi's platform. Therefore, WordPress might also need to hold its assignment as an open supply platform, making sure that each one supply code is shared with whomever might also moreover require it (WPBeginner, 2018).

With each one year of the platform's lifestyles, up to date variations have been released to the general public with modifications designed to make the customer revel in friendlier, as well as to create a platform that would be exciting to apply. For instance, model three.7 have grow to be launched in 2013, and this got here with the automatic software replace characteristic for sites, similar to the manner in which apps are updated on our telephones and computers. In 2018, WordPress introduced the block editor, this is currently used on internet sites in recent times, and changed into given the codename "Gutenberg."

The COVID-19 pandemic delivered number one disruptions for hundreds groups, affecting the WordPress network, too, as they had been not able to meet for awesome WordCamp activities. Here, thoughts for improvements are shared and worked on, similarly to training more people approximately the open source platform as part of the Foundation's mandate. This did no longer have an impact on development, despite the reality that, due to the truth WordPress is a global platform, and lots of its human beings and developers are scattered throughout the globe. Due to this, they had been capable of maintain walking remotely and assembly truely.

During this era, variations five.Four, 5.Five, and 5.6 were launched, with upgrades being made to the automated updates feature, on the component of various internet web site enhancing features. The paintings on the platform keeps, with the following updates to the system forthcoming, and anticipated to be introduced to model 5.Nine, if you want to be launched later in 2022 (WPBeginner, 2018).

Features

WordPress is a multifaceted platform wherein it is simple to assemble a internet site and feature as a CMS too. As such, it wants to have quite a few capabilities so you can entice new customers and hold present day users glad.

Some of the principle abilties that you may find out on the same time as using WordPress are:

Built for All

You can create any form of internet site with WordPress. For instance, you may want to create a personal weblog, a expert blog, a business net internet site, or a photoblog. Whatever your internet web site wishes may be, you'll find out an opportunity and solution that suits you.

WordPress has a large kind of troubles and plugin extensions that will help you layout and create a internet website on your liking. There are subjects and plugins which may be being developed and shared every day through special developers everywhere inside the worldwide.

You might also even assemble your private topics as you pass on growing a website. WordPress changed into created to allow humans with mind have a platform on which to expose off them as nicely, developers and customers alike.

From artwork blogs to on line shopping for websites to government internet websites, they might all be created the use of the WordPress platform. For instance, america President's residence and workplace, The Whitehouse, makes use of WordPress to strength its legit internet website, Whitehouse.Gov. The authentic Microsoft blog is likewise powered thru WordPress, and it has blogs for Windows and Skype that are powered by WordPress as properly (Kinsta, 2018).

Multimedia Management

Any blog internet internet web page or internet website isn't always complete with out pix, films, music, or a few shape of animation. These are key factors that attraction to viewers for your internet website online on-line and maintain it from being silly.

WordPress has a included media library wherein you can preserve all of the unique media formats you need to your internet website. For consolation's sake, you could add your media to the library and upload them to posts, or your internet page in preferred, with out hassle. You can drag and drop pix, and this doesn't require any coding. It is as smooth as posting on social media net websites like Instagram. You also can make a few edits in your snap shots the use of the editor device to be had to you.

User Management

If you run a internet website as a part of an agency or a set of humans, now not every person wishes to have the same manipulate and get proper of entry to to the internet internet page.

You can separate the amount of get entry to you deliver to the designers of the net web page, the writers who submit blogs at the website, and the directors of the internet site online, at the identical time as subscribers should have their private profiles as well. By doing so, you could have severa contributors on your net site, masses inside the equal manner WordPress has developers, and the rest can be a part of your web website online's community.

Application Building

WordPress will let you construct your personal packages if that is some issue that interests you. It is a platform that no longer fine offers you the device to get a mission finished, however wherein you could analyze and pick out out up new skills as well.

From URL routing to databases and HTTP requests, you'll discover most of these equipment and greater on the WordPress platform, as a way to make constructing your non-public apps a satisfaction.

Standard Compliant

All the code created and used inside the WordPress platform is certainly compliant with the requirements set via the World Wide Web Consortium (W3C). The advantage of this is that your internet website will in no manner become obsolete, because it can be continuously maintained to healthful the browsers of the destiny (WordPress, 2018).

Search Engine Optimized

There is not any want to worry approximately people finding your weblog or net website online, for WordPress has an first-rate code base for Search Engine Optimization (search engine optimization). There are numerous plugins associated with seo which might be available to increase your website's visibility.

Importing

Unfortunately no longer all the net website hosting businesses which is probably inside the market will continue to be as such, or you will be unhappy with the services out of your cutting-edge-day software software provider, and consequently you want to transport to WordPress with out losing your web web page and statistics.

The excellent facts is WordPress has importers for Blogger, LiveJournal, Movable Type, TypePad, Tumblr, and, of path, WordPress (WordPress, 2018).

Multilingual

In order to make it on hand to a number of human beings, the WordPress platform has been translated into over 70 languages.

In in many instances, net web sites typically offer a restrained quantity of languages to pick out from, but WordPress permits you to art work in something language you're maximum comfortable with, and moreover makes it a great deal less difficult for traffic for your net internet web page to look at if it may be translated into their close by language.

Compatibility

The technology in smartphones and pills is turning into more superior with each day, and you can advantage greater together with your pocket gadgets. In a few instances, this may consist of converting laptops and computer systems for menial duties like responding to emails.

WordPress is nicely matched with pocket gadgets, making it a whole lot less difficult as a manner to edit your net sites and the content material fabric inner them.

Languages (Codes) Used

For WordPress to feature, it dreams writing

code that is straightforward to evolve and is familiar to builders from all walks of lifestyles. WordPress has a combination of writing language applications, each with a one in all a kind function to it.

These are:

•PHP

•SQL

•HTML

•CSS

•JavaScript

PHP

The critical language utilized by WordPress that makes up its center is Hypertext

Processor (PHP). This is an open source programming and scripting language this is object oriented and used to create dynamic interactive web websites (Technocript, 2021). It is a server-factor language, consequently PHP scripts are performed on the server-issue and despatched to the patron, who only receives to look the outcomes of the code, and not the underlying code that become used.

PHP emerge as created via way of Rasmus Lerdorf in 1994 for web improvement capabilities. It is one of the maximum famous programming languages as it is straightforward to put in and installation, and additionally smooth to investigate. It changed into designed to be used with the useful resource of novices and specialists, which is right for WordPress, as it aims to supply each gadgets of people together, teaching all as they work with the platform.

PHP can be used in the course of all working structures, which include Mac, Windows, or

Linux. Developing an software on one OS and the usage of it on every different OS isn't any trouble, as they may be all incorporated. It is likewise masses faster than many different writing languages available inside the marketplace.

A few examples of the way WordPress makes use of PHP include managing requests to posts and pages; validating permissions that the purchaser has asked, calling plugins, and activating them to do their personal processing (Technocript, 2021).

SQL

Structured Query Language (SQL) is the language used for databases on WordPress. It is a language code that accesses and manipulates databases. Primarily, it have emerge as designed to make it viable to carry out multiple operations and manipulate relational databases.

WordPress calls for 2 key additives for it to run, and that is an utility with scripts and algorithms that address person's requests, and databases used to hold and installation all the records at the website. This includes facts of the customers, posts, and settings. SQL is the database supervisor that the platform makes use of.

HTML

HyperText Markup Language (HTML) isn't a programming language. Instead, it is a markup language used to permit documents to be displayed in a web browser. It is consequently a descriptive markup language wherein content material cloth blocks are created and collocated for the very last internet internet web page.

Every internet web page and net web website online on the internet is an HTML internet net page, which is well ideal with all types of coding languages. WordPress uses HTML for building the structures of pages and posts. The Gutenberg net web page builder brought in 2018 on the WordPress platform makes it a good deal less complicated as a manner to look and regulate HTML code in every content material material material block.

CSS

Cascading Styling Sheets (CSS) artwork on the side of HTML to give your page its final look. CSS is a styling language you use at the same time as describing the visible look of components inside an HTML record.

It lets you fashion the HTML structure however you need, on the aspect of your creativity being the handiest limit. You can role your paragraph to the left, and exchange the colour of the text or the history. You can change font length, type, and add spaces to the brink of your internet web page, too, if you so want.

WordPress is based totally on CSS for its troubles, and it's miles those state of affairs subjects that make up the visible look of your net website. Every taken into consideration considered one of them, therefore, has a style.Css file that controls the visible look of your net website online on line.

Javascript

One programming language you're sure to come upon in all aspects of programming is Javascript (JS). It permits for the client to engage with the internet website online and makes digital content cloth greater interactive, in giant.

Javascript is a consumer-facet programming language and no longer like PHP, it does no longer require a server to be processed, as it runs right now at the character's browser. It can change the style of a particular HTML element, display or conceal an element, and set rely variety-down timers, and an entire lot extra.

WordPress makes use of Javascript to function dynamic behavior to pages and posts, as maximum of the hassle topics and plugins at the platform use JS for particular abilities and dynamic factors to pages and posts.

Learning to use CSS, HTML, and Javascript will offer you with the critical know-how units and base knowledge in your internet development journey, and it makes it much less complex to apprehend PHP, as they may be all nicely appropriate and used at the facet of each different.

Chapter 17: Benefits And Drawbacks Of Wordpress

There are different internet web web site-constructing systems available in the marketplace like Shopify, Wix, Weebly, Joomla, and Magento. Each of these serves a unique reason for superb internet web sites.

For example, you may use Magento and Shopify to create an eCommerce internet internet website online for on line purchasing and so on, however you'll not use the equal packages to create a weblog after which convert it into an internet keep. They lack that form of versatility, and this is wherein WordPress scores factors, and is some of the motives why it's far one of the most famous website building structures to be had.

Although WordPress is famous with the masses, it can not satisfy every person's desires all of the time. It has its benefits and its pitfalls too, and in advance than you embark on a adventure of gaining knowledge of to use it, it's miles awesome to remember every sides of the coin.

Benefits

When gauging the brilliant of a services or products, we usually need the exceptional to outweigh the horrible. Some of the advantages/blessings of WordPress are:

Open Source Platform

WordPress is unfastened to apply due to the fact it is an open supply CMS and net website online-constructing platform. This manner that every one the code that you use inside the platform is open for sharing and exchange with the resource of the usage of in reality absolutely everyone, and you do not need to build your code from scratch.

The codes for plugins and venture subjects at the platform are underneath the GPLv2 license and are unfastened. There are no licenses or subscription costs that you want to pay at the same time as the use of or improving the code.

Having a big community inside the platform manner there are extra mind being shared, and so you will spend a good deal less time seeking to beautify your codes with each challenge, because of the truth the platform makes it convenient if you want to combine your contemporary code with new codes which can be being advanced all the time (Souvik, 2021). The WordPress community is there to useful resource you even as you get caught or have hassle reading and using the device at the platform.

Plugins

WordPress is an All-in-one platform that caters to all your internet site-building desires, however it does not have all of the extended capabilities available in its database.

Furthermore, with a huge and numerous developer network, there are normally new abilities that can be added, and that is in which plugins come into play. A primary advantage of the use of WordPress is that it has a plethora of plugins you could use to beautify the capability of your internet site. From heightening the safety of your internet web page to look plugins that could decorate the visible trouble of your net web page, you may find out a plugin a very good manner to give you the outcomes you want.

You can upload social media widgets to boom verbal exchange in your clients and or the agencies to your web sites, upload junk mail control abilties, or use plugins like Google Analytics to show the general overall performance of your net website and make the essential changes to enhance the net website.

User Friendly

You do now not want to be a developer or hire a developer to make a website for your self using WordPress. The platform is straightforward to put in and navigate round. Learning to use the interface will no longer consume too much of some time, and getting improvements is problem-free, as masses of them update robotically on the platform and in your websites.

Editing and together with content material in your net web web site has been made a lot less complicated the use of WordPress, while you recollect that you could drag and drop content material material, and navigate via topics and text blocks without the want for expert technical knowledge.

search engine marketing and advertising Compatible

Having made a internet site, you need it to be seen and less difficult to locate on the internet, specially with the innumerable different websites available. Trying to pick the right keywords in your content or meta titles and meta descriptions isn't always an clean assignment. It is difficult to try and determine those out with out an outdoor score device.

WordPress makes it much less complex on the consumer, because it has gadget that help you pick out commonplace phrases and terms which you may use to growth the visibility of your weblog or net web site (Khan, 2018). For instance, when you have a weblog about basketball, then you can look for the most generally used and searched phrases and terms regarding basketball on the net, thereby setting those to your headings and content. This will assist boom your internet web site online's score and be much less complex to find out even as those words are searched in any internet browser.

User Management

Not simplest does WordPress offer you with an option to separate the jobs of the administrators and individuals in your website on-line, it gives you whole control of your net web web page, in addition to what others can do in it. You very own all of the information at the internet web site and might manipulate what appears for your website, together with classified ads.

You can show and function manage of your net web page notwithstanding the reality that it has a problem with the code. This may be completed through using SiteHealth, a undertaking which changed into brought into the tool in 2019 to assist deal with problems of older PHP code, and by way of giving the patron notifications to update even as those are detected. It comes with a further layer of projection, because it permits you to safely log in for your internet page at the same time as there can be a crucial mistakes and attach the problem from within the dashboard (WPBeginner, 2021a).

Drawbacks

Like all subjects in existence, not some thing is quality, and the equal is genuine for internet websites. No depend how hard we try, we cannot a hundred% assure that some element will paintings at complete capacity all of the time.

Technical troubles will arise proper here and there. For the ones reasons, we want to be privy to the one of a kind conditions in which WordPress falls short.

Mediocre search engine optimization Ranking

Although WordPress offers seo talents on its platform, they'll be not enough enough to advantage a respectable score on Google, and therefore they received't do masses to your internet site on line's visibility.

You will need to are looking for out the offerings of seo expert groups to be able to maximize your search engine advertising endeavors and outrank the numerous wonderful web websites on the internet. When deciding on an search engine optimization expert, make certain to pick out out those that target lots of key phrases, as most handiest attention on a handful of key phrases, and this does not assist a whole lot in getting your internet web website online ranked (Souvik, 2021).

Numerous Plugins for Extra Features

It is a top notch component that WordPress is nicely matched with a massive variety of plugins which can be to be had to be had available on the market. The problem is, however, the want for a number of these plugins.

When you buy a design template, it comes with completely designed pages and a internet site that you will be looking to feature your content material to, which incorporates your logos and brand schemes. For all the extra functions you may want to characteristic for your net web site, you can need plugins for the ones.

Some plugins are available at the WordPress platform, and you could attain those freed from charge, but for masses of those you could must get them externally—generally coming with a fee. For example, you may need a widget for every of the social media systems you want to connect to your net site.

Purchasing those plugins might also even require you to install them, manage them, and additionally preserve them updated, and this could be a problem, subsequently why many companies pull away from obtaining the ones (Doctorlogic, 2022).

Frequent Updates

With all of the extra troubles and plugins established to your internet site, they may require protection, and this comes in the shape of updating them. As masses as your internet website updates with each improve that is made available, your plugins require the identical movement, in any other case they will not be properly matched with the greater contemporary software software on your internet website. This can corrupt the plugin skills, slowing them down or resulting in them being obsolete, if you want to have an impact on the general overall performance and functionality of your internet web page.

www.ingramcontent.com/pod-product-compliance
Lightning Source LLC
La Vergne TN
LVHW022315060326
832902LV00020B/3482